Quality Experience Telemetry

Also available from ASQ Quality Press:

Achieving Customer Experience Excellence through a Quality Management System
Alka Jarvis, Luis Morales, and Ulka Ranadive

Navigating the Minefield: A Practical KM Companion
Patricia Lee Eng and Paul J. Corney

The Certified Software Quality Engineer Handbook, Second Edition
Linda Westfall

Introduction to 8D Problem Solving: Including Practical Applications and Examples
Ali Zarghami and Don Benbow

The Quality Toolbox, Second Edition
Nancy R. Tague

Root Cause Analysis: Simplified Tools and Techniques, Second Edition
Bjørn Andersen and Tom Fagerhaug

The Certified Six Sigma Green Belt Handbook, Second Edition
Roderick A. Munro, Govindarajan Ramu, and Daniel J. Zrymiak

The Certified Manager of Quality/Organizational Excellence Handbook, Fourth Edition
Russell T. Westcott, editor

The Certified Six Sigma Black Belt Handbook, Third Edition
T. M. Kubiak and Donald W. Benbow

The ASQ Auditing Handbook, Fourth Edition
J. P. Russell, editor

The ASQ Quality Improvement Pocket Guide: Basic History, Concepts, Tools, and Relationships
Grace L. Duffy, editor

To request a complimentary catalog of ASQ Quality Press publications, call 800-248-1946, or visit our website at http://www.asq.org/quality-press.

Quality Experience Telemetry

How to Effectively Use Telemetry for Improved Customer Success

Alka Jarvis, Luis Morales, and Johnson Jose

ASQ Quality Press
Milwaukee, Wisconsin

American Society for Quality, Quality Press, Milwaukee 53203
© 2018 by ASQ
All rights reserved.
Printed in the United States of America
23 22 21 20 19 18   5 4 3 2 1

Library of Congress Cataloging-in-Publication Data
Names: Jarvis, Alka, author.
Title: Quality experience telemetry : how to effectively use telemetry for improved
    customer success / Alka Jarvis, Luis Morales, and Johnson Jose.
Description: Milwaukee, Wis. : ASQ Quality Press, [2018]
Identifiers: LCCN 2018001111 | ISBN 9780873899673 (hardcover : alk. paper)
Subjects: LCSH: Customer relations—Quality control. | Customer services—Technological
    innovations. | Telematics.
Classification: LCC HF5415.5 .J373 2018 | DDC 658.8/12—dc23
LC record available at https://lccn.loc.gov/2018001111

Director, Quality Press and Programs: Ray Zielke
Managing Editor: Paul Daniel O'Mara
Sr. Creative Services Specialist: Randy L. Benson

ASQ Mission: The American Society for Quality advances individual, organizational, and community excellence worldwide through learning, quality improvement, and knowledge exchange.

Attention Bookstores, Wholesalers, Schools, and Corporations: ASQ Quality Press books, video, audio, and software are available at quantity discounts with bulk purchases for business, educational, or instructional use. For information, please contact ASQ Quality Press at 800-248-1946, or write to ASQ Quality Press, P.O. Box 3005, Milwaukee, WI 53201–3005.

To place orders or to request a free copy of the ASQ Quality Press Publications Catalog, visit our website at http://www.asq.org/quality-press.

 Printed on acid-free paper

Quality Press
600 N. Plankinton Ave.
Milwaukee, WI 53203-2914
E-mail: authors@asq.org
The Global Voice of Quality®

Table of Contents

List of Figures and Tables

Foreword

The notion of telemetry, the capacity to access remote data quickly, has, indeed, been around, as the authors point out, for a long time. With advancing technological capabilities becoming a robust reality, there are numerous ways of gathering data, fast ways to analyze it, and an ever-increasing capacity to expand the type of data and sources that can be mobilized. This capacity opens immense and important opportunities. While we have an ability to gather information quickly, this ability in and of itself is meaningless unless we know why we are actually gathering it and understand the particular problems we are trying to solve. Data can blind us unless we know what we're looking for. Without a framing perspective, the data we gather accomplishes little.

This book does just that for the field of customer service. The authors have done something remarkable, in my opinion. They've asked, first and foremost, what are the critical organizational behavior questions that need to be answered and, in turn, what are the systems, processes, and software that can be employed to answer those questions.

This is an important and timely book. Students of organizational behavior for the last 15 years have been asking how to integrate the technology of data gathering and data analysis with critical organizational challenges. This book shows how to do that, using the field of customer service to illustrate the broader point.

In recent years, much has been written about the value of having deeper relationships with customers. This is especially true, as the authors point out, in the area of customer retention. How does an organization establish a continuous relationship that is agile, scalable, and responsive to customer needs? Selling a product or solution at one point in time is never enough. We must continuously monitor customer challenges, problems, and needs. The challenge is obvious. What is the best and most cost-efficient way to ensure this? How can we establish a proactive relationship with customers that ensures their retention, fulfills their expectations, and, all in all, establishes a "top-class customer experience"?

At its core, to my mind, this volume provides a blueprint to doing just that, and does so in a clear fashion. Specifically, this volume allows lay readers to understand telemetry and helps them enhance their data-gathering activities to strengthen customer relations. It gives the readers the tools they need to ensure continuous improvement and adjustments to enhance the customer relationship. It suggests modes of analysis to identify critical problems and their causes. In addition, it gives the reader the perspective to create and develop actionable responses.

In many ways, this book serves as a critical venue to introduce tools, constructs, concepts, and methodologies that allow leaders in contemporary organizations to make sure they have the systems in place to read both the strong and weak signals that suggest a need to make adjustments, take steps, or further elaborate on a particular problem. In today's complex world, without having these tools, it is no longer possible for one organization, one unit, or one department to monitor the customer's environment and stay ahead of customer aspirations.

In a world where we would like to be able to operate in real-time as much as possible and where it is essential that we stay agile to stay ahead of the competition, the very notion of telemetry, not simply as a technology but as a mindset, is essential. This volume makes this evident and concrete.

Samuel B. Bacharach
McKelvey-Grant Professor, Cornell University, New York
Founder, Bacharach Leadership Group, and author of 20 leadership books

Preface

The authors of this book have been working for one of Silicon Valley's premier technology companies for more than a decade. During this time, we have all served in different roles and capacities including software engineering, customer assurance, quality management, and technology development and implementation. However, our paths have repeatedly intersected in the area of quality management and we have witnessed how the latest technology/market transitions around the Internet of Things, digitization, and telemetry are impacting the company we work with, the high-tech industry, and the global economy. On multiple occasions, we have met and discussed how exciting, significant, and potentially transformational these changes will be to the way companies do quality management and drive continuous improvement in customer experience. Ultimately, a decision was made by us to write a book that would explore these opportunities in more detail.

Specifically, this book is dedicated to the study of telemetry data and its potential use to drive continuous improvement in customer experience. The real-time nature of the data and the advent of machine-learning algorithms have set the stage for a new era we call *adaptive customer experience*. The premise of this concept is that real-time availability of customer experience data opens the door for real-time responses based on predeployed machine-learning algorithms. This is creating an unprecedented opportunity to change the relationship between customers and the systems they depend on in their digital world.

Why is real-time quality data availability such a big deal? To understand, you must realize that most data used today to measure customer experience comes from analysis of customer calls. Customer call data gets processed typically once a month, at which point it is used to update downstream metrics. Depending on the metric, a statistically significant change in trend will not raise an alert unless it happens for at least two reporting cycles (two months) in a row. At this point, one is lagging at least two months from the moment the customer experienced the pain that triggered the call. Additionally, factors such as metric normalization (e.g., install base) prevent metrics from reacting to small changes. Analogous to turning a large ship versus a small boat, strategic metrics won't move unless a significant portion of the install base is experiencing a problem. So again, data based on customer calls will not trigger a systemic corrective action until the problem becomes more pervasive.

In addition to real-time responses based on algorithms, there is still a need for some of the data collected through telemetry to be sent and shared with software vendors in order to drive more systemic improvements. Today, companies tend to tailor their business operations around quarterly business reviews (QBRs). These forums occur at different levels within a company and are designed to prepare and review the information needed to create financial reports to investors. Customer experience and quality data is typically reviewed in QBR forums and the monthly/quarterly cycle time of data refresh fits nicely into that business cadence.

With the advent of real-time customer experience data, there is an opportunity to consume the information differently and accelerate time to action. A path to achieve that builds on the concept of digitization but specifically focuses on operational processes targeting quality. We call those processes *critical-to-quality processes*. If we target those processes that are critical to quality first, we are enabling the company to consume/respond to customer experience faster than ever. Customer support and customer listening are good examples of critical-to-quality processes being targeted for digitization today.

In this book, we use customer success as an example of a business model that is highly dependent on telemetry data. This model is being widely adopted by software and service companies. The idea behind this is to get the salesforce to think about a broader customer life cycle that includes adoption, renewal, and refresh, in addition to the traditional sale. Customer success and customer experience are highly intertwined so it is important to understand differences and similarities.

Finally, we get into use cases and applications that bring telemetry to life for the business. In our increasingly digitized world, the proliferation of sensors and improvement in data science capabilities create an environment where possibilities for telemetry are limitless. Imagination is the only ingredient that needs to be added to turn telemetry data into valuable insights for people and businesses across the global economy.

A successful telemetry-driven customer experience improvement program requires a strong foundation in:

1. *Quality.* You need to have a strong foundation in quality and quality management principles. These principles include but are not limited to definition of metrics, customer listening, and root cause analysis. The establishment of quality governance forums is a best practice to ensure insights turn into actions. Change management and approaches to create sustainability of improvements are also foundational.

2. *Data.* Leveraging telemetry requires a solid foundation of knowledge of data, so it is important to have a good understanding of basic data structures, organizational approaches, database types, and big data. It is also important to understand the basic concepts behind data quality and data security. Companies are making large capital investments in building the infrastructure required to support telemetry. It is important to understand the basic elements of that infrastructure and how to best interact with it to extract data.

3. *People.* From a people perspective, data scientists are key players in the telemetry field. They have the necessary mastery of underlying data principles needed to implement telemetry programs. They will not only help create the necessary infrastructure to collect, house, and manage telemetry data, but also will drive efforts to turn data into actionable insights.

With the above in mind, the book is organized into six chapters:

- Chapter 1 introduces concepts that will be referenced and built on later in the book such as customer satisfaction, customer retention, customer experience, customer expectations, and so on. Additionally, some of today's technology trends like digitization, Internet of Things as telemetry, cloud computing, machine learning, and artificial intelligence are introduced. These trends serve as catalysts for the emergence of telemetry data and they are driving changes in customer expectations, value delivery, and business models across industries.

- Chapter 2 describes what telemetry is, why telemetry is needed, and what it accomplishments it provides.

- Chapter 3 walks the reader through the evolutionary journey of data science from its humble beginnings to present uses of telemetry data in creating adaptive experiences.

- Chapter 4 elaborates on how telemetry can be used to create a software development organization that is more responsive and efficient at meeting customer needs.

- Chapter 5 focuses on the skills and capabilities needed to build and sustain "telemetry enabled organizations." We also review various technology options on the market that can be leveraged to realize a telemetry infrastructure and to accelerate the workforce transformation.

- Chapter 6 summarizes the salient points of the book and dives further into concepts like digitization that are impacting/disrupting companies across the world economy. We close with a checklist that would help organizations looking to engage in the business of creating, consuming, or processing data telemetry.

Acknowledgments

We are pleased to present *Quality Experience Telemetry: How to Effectively Use Telemetry for Improved Customer Success*. The book provides necessary knowledge and information to understand the telemetry infrastructure and associated details. This will enable readers to implement telemetry, in order to address customer pains and successfully deploy techniques to improve customer experience.

We have been fortunate to have several subject matter experts on telemetry give their time and knowledge to make the contents robust. Our special thanks goes to Satabhish Aeka for his tremendous contributions in Chapter 2. We recognize Pete Rotella and Carol Candelaria for their advice and input on Chapter 3, and Deepak Adiga for his insights in creating the telemetry ecosystem as well as the introduction to technology landscape. In addition, Karthic Balasubramani shared valuable knowledge in software organizational behavior and agile practices.

This book would not have been possible without the leadership and support of our production editor, Paul Daniel O'Mara. Our sincere thanks to him for his ongoing encouragement and guidance.

1

Introduction

It is extremely costly to get a new customer on board and ensure that customer does not leave. The marketing team has to do a lot of work to create advertisements that will draw consumer attention. The sales team has to work equally hard to set up meetings with potential interested parties, meet with them, and confirm the contract is signed. This may require multiple visits from the sales representative to the customer site. In the event the customer is located in another state or city, associated travel and living expenses are incurred. Once the contract is finalized, ensuring the new customer has adequate knowledge to start using your product requires effort. If the company has a training department, then training has to be set up, and this, too, adds to the cost.

As soon as the customer is acquired, the challenge is to retain that customer. Oftentimes, issues concerning the product only surface once the customer begins using the product. Listening to the problems encountered by the customer via methods such as a yearly survey is no longer an option. With *telemetry*—the touted technology—collecting product usage data from customers is an efficient way to understand customer pain points. It is one of the most powerful methods of understanding the behavior of the product in the hands of the users, recognizing associated difficulties, and proactively contacting the customer with a fix or a solution.

Along with telemetry, there are also other elements that need consideration for keeping customers happy and increasing their retention. These should all be strategically inserted in your company's business model and there should be people assigned to address them. We will provide insights on each of these elements:

- Business models

- Customer satisfaction

- Time to market

- Customer experience

- Customer expectations

- Technological tipping points for productivity and growth

- Proactive, corrective, and preventive improvements

- Telemetry

- Disruptions due to digital trends

- Continuous improvements

- Proactive versus corrective and preventive

- Change management

1.1 BUSINESS MODELS

Individuals must have a thorough understanding of their company's business model. Global companies that are technical and digital leaders view their business model as crucial for meeting their strategic goals. There is an ongoing struggle for many to understand the concept of a business model, and *business model* often appears to be some vague technical term. It can be easily understood, however, if broken down into three simple items: the plans the company has to generate revenue, the approaches the company has to retain the customers, and the operational strategies that will enable the company to sustain its business and remain profitable. There are other elements that are added to the model based on new competitive threats, changing customer needs, the customer value proposition, or new business opportunities. *Value proposition* describes the benefits a customer gets by using your company's products or services. The greater value the customer gets, the more inclination there is for additional purchases. A computer company may start business by offering software for payroll. If the demand of this payroll package increases, the business model may have to change to accommodate more customers, additional marketing, and training or selling the payroll package internationally. In addition to the original payroll package, the company may decide to add some consulting services along with an expanded payroll package for companies, including data entry, check printing, direct bank deposits, and so on.

Your company's business model indicates the type of customers on whom to focus sales strategies, customer preservation tactics, as well as the support services formulated to target these customers. If the research and development (R&D) department identifies different types of customers who would be interested in the same product, then the company will change the business model to accommodate the newly identified customer base.

As the market evolves and your company decides the model it is following is no longer favorable, you will be forced to change the model to develop new strategies that will be beneficial. This is the period in which a first-class customer experience (CX) through digital experience (DX) can be provided—and telemetry fits into this plan. We see business leaders review their strategies and models frequently so they can remain at the forefront of their customers' minds when it comes time for them to repurchase a product. Decisions to change are driven by customer perception and what is happening in the marketplace and not by mere discussions in a board meeting or a conference room. With the increased interconnectivity between countries and quicker time frames to develop and take products to the market, many companies update their business models periodically, but with the increased focus on CX and DX, the business models are changing at a rapid-fire pace. Successful changes in business models are driven by hard-core telemetry data, which is collected and analyzed. A sudden change is detrimental to any business; therefore, care in changing to the new model, while still supporting the current one, is a desirable method for recognized innovators.

Innovative leaders are more prepared to review, evaluate, tweak, or replace a model to please customers, increase the fluidity of revenue, increase brand recognition, be known as a "market leader," or be rated number one for top customer satisfaction scores. Let us further explore the saturation of new technologies and the shifting attitudes of customers and their needs to get a better perspective about the strong necessity to alter the business models often.

1.2 CUSTOMER SATISFACTION

The term *customer satisfaction* is used frequently, and everyone has his or her own meaning for it. If we were to summarize the meaning, it is a marketing expression that measures how products supplied meet or surpass a customer's experience or expectation; it is an important element that plays a role in the sustained success of an organization. Leaders across many companies have indicated that measuring customer satisfaction has assisted them in measuring and monitoring their business, but this is just a starting point.

1.2.1 Retention of Customers

Building an ongoing relationship with the customer to encourage the retention rate requires special efforts. To build this relationship, there are small activities that will yield better results, such as:

- Use of blogs to educate customers on existing and new functionalities.

- One-on-one meeting with customers to get their feedback. Note that this can become a costly proposition; our experience indicates that companies will adopt the 80/20 rule, meaning that 80% of the business is generated by 20% of the customer base. These are the customers who will be contacted for one-on-one meetings. Companies that have built trust through one-on-one relationships have gained market share and have lost very few top revenue-generating customers.

- Traditional once-a-year customer satisfaction surveys have become obsolete. For example, a customer may have been very unhappy with the product, but when completing the survey five or six months later, the urgency to provide feedback has dissipated so the feedback may not reflect the real pain the customer experienced at the time of purchase. For this reason, we now see "just-in-time" surveys, where the incidents are still fresh in the customer's mind and the feedback provided is based on the true experience. Just-in-time or transaction-based surveys enable businesses to address product-related problems almost immediately, thereby preventing any negative press or media attention.

- Customized products take the customer satisfaction several notches higher. Just imagine that you have gone to a new restaurant for dinner and you find out that due to your dietary restrictions, there is nothing on the menu that you can order. Yet, the waiter hears your story and gives you several different options of ordering a personalized meal that the chef will prepare just for you. Can you think of your delight at the news of this customized service? Your satisfaction will automatically escalate. To stay ahead of the market curve, we see companies offering personalized solutions to their customers, thus increasing the retention rate by a much higher percentage. Personalization lets the customers know that you are not addressing them as a "mass crowd" but as an "individual," whose preferences and choices matter.

Taking interest in the success of your customers by allocating a small portion of your budget to better know them and find ways to assist them will go a long way toward retaining those customers. Simply providing a product is no longer the end goal. Spending time to find out how you can provide a meaningful product that meets your customer's needs should provide better leverage when the customer must decide to stay with you or go to some other vendor.

Retention is a far more proficient method to increase sales and increase the financial bottom line than continually reaching out for new customers. Once the customer decides to stay with your company, it may still be difficult to focus on actions and results based on the customers' feedback because customer expectations literally change on daily basis. Just relying on the old cliché of "keep your customer satisfied" does not work in today's ever-changing environment with its increased customer demands. Today's consumers are very savvy about what they want, how they want to be treated, and how much they are willing to pay for a product. With constantly shifting business and economic, as well as social environments, customer satisfaction has become a journey and not a final destination. The focus needs to be on *anticipatory service*, which can be construed as proactively identifying customer expectations instead of waiting for the customer to come to you with a request—that is, you identify what the customer expects and strategically develop a proactive approach to customer service. Proactive approach means customer loyalty and stronger customer relationships because you are performing your due diligence in identifying customer requirements or eliminating problems before they occur by analyzing telemetry data, thus contributing to increased customer experience.

Here are some of the examples of anticipatory services:

- A customer is sent a fix to a product's problem before it is encountered

- A mail order pharmacy notifies the customer when the next prescription refill will be mailed

- An airline notifies the customers ahead of time when there is a gate change

- A doctor's office calls the patient one month ahead of time when regular yearly check-up is due

- A bank alerts a customer ahead of time when his bank balance is low and an incoming check is about to be rejected

- A vendor notifies the customer when the next payment is due

1.3 TIME TO MARKET

In one of his interviews, Howard Schultz, chief executive officer (CEO) of Starbucks, stated that he would rather be first to market with a new product than have a perfect product. Why would he say this? What is the logic? First to market is important because being late erodes your opportunities to capture the market. The smaller market means fewer sales and less revenue. Decreased time to reach the market allows your competitors to capture consumers before you have a chance to market them, thus allowing competitors to dominate the market and become market leaders.

Being first to go to the market with a product provides recognition and a chance to capture the attention of the media as well as potential buyers' attention. Because you are the first to show the products to consumers, you will be the first to receive beneficial feedback on enhancements and new functionalities to be added. You can also continue to excel by providing product-related training, seminars, and special licensed support (which generates extra revenue).

One of the challenges faced, however, is this: how does your company identify prospects, capitalize on them, and take calculated risks? Identifying risks and planning mitigation up front can augment your chances and control major failures. There are several ways to increase your market reach:

- *Anticipate needs of your customers.* Companies have deployed various techniques to get feedback from customers in order to stay a step ahead. Despite new methodologies, the old rule of 80/20 that we discussed earlier in the chapter still applies. The rule also advocates having a strong relationship with the 20% of your customers from whom 80% of your business is coming, in order to get new ideas on what these customers would like to see in your products. You may want to have face-to-face meetings or form a customer advisory committee that meets on a quarterly basis to discuss the product functionalities, issues, and future enhancements or solutions your customers are looking for.

  User group meetings still remain the most popular channel for identifying the needs of customers and obtaining ideas for the user base. In either of the methods—a customer advisory committee or user group meetings—you have to be diligent to capture all the ideas and notify the attendees on a continuous basis as to how the ideas and issues discussed in a meeting are addressed. Frequent communication with the user group attendees forms a loyal customer base that is eager to share helpful innovative concepts connected to the products.

- *Research and development.* R&D is a functional organization in your company that works toward the advancement of your products, processes, technologies, etc. It plays a major role in the process of innovation and future capabilities, which can be converted into new products or services. R&D is a key element in developing new competitive advantages. A robust research department continuously monitors domestic and international markets to look for product ideas, building prototypes, and evaluating the marketing feasibility.

  When it comes to R&D, the name of Intel comes to mind. Through constant R&D, this massive company is way ahead of its competition and has a major market share. Its large investment in R&D enables the company to ship new and better products faster than its competitors. Through its technology, Intel claims: "We believe technology must constantly evolve to make more things possible and all things easier, smarter, and more connected than ever before," thus remaining a market leader.

1.4 CUSTOMER EXPERIENCE

Customer experience (CX) has a complex definition. It is the combined interaction among a customer, the product, and the company. This interaction occurs over the duration of the relationship between the company and the customer and also over the life of the product. The interaction between the customer and company, whether direct or indirect, also plays a role in the customer experience. These interactions may be little details the customer remembers when interacting with the company and/or its website, marketing campaigns, salespeople, support people, etc. These are the details that made the customer happy originally and enabled the decision to buy from you and remain with you.

CX has a direct relationship to the customer loyalty and is very closely tied to it. Pleasant, unexpected, and memorable experiences influence the customer to become your dedicated consumer.

1.4.1 Common CX Attributes

- *Attention to detail.* The golden rule is that anything that touches the customer should be defect free and that all related documentation must be tested to ensure it is written in language that can be understood by all customers, regardless of educational background. For this reason, the words "user friendly" have gained extensive popularity since the early 1980s. To be *user friendly* means the customer will not have to struggle to understand the user manuals or to start using the product.

  Companies such as IBM and others are known to have established usability labs to learn about user experiences on the products they sell. Usability can be defined as:
  — Easy to learn
  — Easy to use

— Easy to remember
— Less frustrating for the user to finish a task
— The ability to quickly recover from errors

Before buying a new product, we all depend on the internet. If your company's website is hard to navigate and the contents are hard to understand, a potential buyer will be turned off immediately and go to some other company's website, where the data is easy to understand and the website is user friendly. Design considerations to make the website intuitive will encourage customers to spend more time studying the contents and help them make a quick decision.

- *Sensitivity.* As alluded to earlier, conducting business requires cultivating relationships and maintaining them. To maintain a positive relationship, you need to be sensitive to the requirements and needs of the customer. The customer is an individual with personal needs, which cannot be downplayed. Simple consideration goes a long way. Here are two examples:
  — At the end of a flight, the pilot or stewardess makes an announcement: "We know you have other choices of flying, and we appreciate your choosing our airline. We hope to see you again on another flight."
  — A salesperson lets the customer know that there is a cheaper option he or she can purchase, rather than the one they are looking at, that could save them money.

  Understanding sensitivity falls under having "soft skills," which involves politeness and handling customer's emotional status. The use of the right words and caring may prevent a lost sale. Many companies are updating the knowledge base of their employees to include training on cultural and sensitivity aspects of understanding the customer and treating each situation differently, as well as paying attention to understanding the power of positive impression on the customer.

- *Gratitude.* The saying "customer is always right" or "customer is the king" says it all. Encouraging all employees to show gratitude toward the customer base is paramount. Never forget that there may be many other businesses such as yours from which the customer can purchase similar products. To show appreciation for their loyalty is a value-added benefit. For this reason, many companies now have their customer support person end a customer call with "We value your business!"

- *Delight.* CX is really delighting your customer with the next best thing in a product by continually paying attention to innovation and developing something that absolutely takes the breath away! Apple and Amazon come to mind when talking about delighting the customer. Both companies' successes have been astonishing. Through innovation and customer delight, Apple has taken over the market previously dominated by the BlackBerry, and Apple is selling new versions of iPhones as soon as they come to the market. Amazon has far exceeded customer delight by providing an easy way for consumers to order and a failure-proof, timely method of delivery. The firms that pay attention to delighting their customers constantly compete on time and get the products faster to the market.

Note that one of the jobs of R&D is to find out what the customer really needs or anticipate what the customer will want, thus delighting him or her. Think about Apple's success. It has shown that it is not always a "need," but also a "fancy" that your company can fulfill. Apple has brought products such as the iPod, iPhone, iPad, and iTunes to the market, all of which succeeded in getting people excited and enthusiastic to buy, and Apple has kept a large market share by being the first to offer many of the products, confirming what we have said before about the criticality of time to market.

The added benefit is that companies that delight their customers have to spend less money in marketing because their customers will do part of the job for them by singing their praises to their friends in person and on social media.

- *Automation.* Automating certain activities to interact with your customers will save time and enhance the experience. Activities such as ordering, viewing past orders, or providing functionality for the customers to view order status provides a way for customers to stay up-to-date on their orders. The trick is to automate without sacrificing the personal touch. Automation avoids human errors, provides consistent results each time, and improves communications.

  Training plays an important role in the customer's comfort level in using automation. Ensure that you have provided adequate training and provided cheat sheets and user manuals for reference. For easy access to the training, you can develop VODs (videos on demand) that can be accessed by the users any time, thereby having the information at their fingertips.

- *Use of social media.* With easy internet access and information availability, your customers are spending more and more time online. Social media is more pervasive than ever, and using tools such as LinkedIn, Facebook, Twitter, and others for ongoing communications pays high returns on investment. More than 2 billion users around the globe rely on social media for news or updates, and this number is increasing as access to internet becomes easier and cheaper.

  In 2016, a report by the Pew Research Center stated 62% of social media users get news through social media platforms. This percentage was up from 49% four years earlier. The report also stated, "Facebook is by far the largest social networking site, reaching 67% of U.S. adults. The two-thirds of Facebook users who get news there, then, amount to 44% of the general population."[1] Ongoing briefing related to your products offered, success stories of the use of the product, interviews with the users, and news about the next promotion assist in relationship building.

When customers consistently receive beneficial news, it helps develop loyalty.

- *Fingered speech.* You may never have heard this term before. However, you have seen tweets or received many text messages, which are typed by fingers—thus the name, "fingered speech." In the same manner, sending e-mails or receiving them also classifies as fingered speech. Individuals who write either on Facebook or on Twitter leave data trails that are electronic. These trails can be gathered and analyzed. In these media, people say what they want to express themselves. Believe it or not, for many, this form of communication through finger speech has become a daily routine. For family members who are located worldwide, fingered speech is the main mode of communication they have selected to keep in touch with their loved ones.

  John McWhorter, who has given several TED talks about linguistics, indicated that texting operates less like the language of writing than the language of speaking. So, through "fingered" speech, a text message can go from one person to the next with the speed of lightning. Why are we talking about texting in a chapter that is outlining customer needs and technologies that affect companies to better serve the customer? Well, the most critical way of marketing a product is through "word of mouth." Armed with dissatisfaction with a company, a customer can do a lot of damage by describing the experience through fingered speech.

  Customer listening and satisfaction metrics are huge topics in and of themselves, and we cover them in well-deserved detail in Chapter 3.

We just highlighted the key activities that play a role in customer experience and complement your efforts to rely on telemetry data. We now discuss how customer expectation, when met, has tremendous power to influence customer loyalty to a given company.

1.5 CUSTOMER EXPECTATIONS

There is a strong difference between customer experience and customer expectations. *Customer experience* is an interpretation of the collective encounters a customer has from the time he or she decides to buy your product to the time it is purchased, used, and supported. *Customer expectation* is an assumption made while purchasing a product. To understand customer expectations, you have to know your customer profiles to understand who they are, what they need now, and what they will need in the future. The product provided by you—which may be hardware, software, or service—must meet current needs; however, if that product becomes obsolete in a year, you are not going to have repeat business. Customers are loyal to the companies that, on an ongoing basis, fulfill their needs and help run their business smoothly by providing state-of-art products and then continually enhancing these products to meet ongoing demands due to economic or consumer changes.

Expectation and experience go hand-in-hand. If a customer's high expectations fall short, his or her experience will be affected, which will have a domino effect on satisfaction. These three have a triangular relationship, and as shown in Figure 1.1, you cannot separate them.

Customer expectations set a high bar and affect future buying decisions. If you have met and exceeded the bar, the customer is more likely to come back for the next purchase and also refer you to friends or post positive comments on social media. There are a few simple steps to knowing customer expectations:

- Understand your customer profile:
  - Who is the customer (e.g., large companies, small companies, individuals)?
  - What is the demographic? Is it a domestic or global company?
  - What is the size of the company?
  - Who is the decision maker?
  - What is the customer's capacity in terms of dollars?
  - How did the customer start its purchasing efforts and where/who did it reach out to?
  - What is the customer's familiarity with the products you are offering or with related technology?
  - How is the customer using the product?
  - How often does the customer call your customer support?
  - How much businesses have your received from the customer in the last three to five years?
  - How fast is the customer's business growing?
  - If it is an individual buyer, what age group does the customer belongs to?

We have also seen companies develop customer personas in addition to customer profiles. The word *persona* is used differently in the industry. For some, a persona is a representation of an ideal customer based on market research and real data about existing customers. In this instance, once pertinent customer data has been gathered, the company will be in a position to develop strategies to not only meet customer's needs but to exceed their expectations. In others, persona is used for roles and responsibilities of individuals within the company.

Figure 1.1 Triangular relationship.

1.6 TECHNOLOGICAL TIPPING POINTS FOR PRODUCTIVITY AND GROWTH

Along with telemetry, many of the technologies mentioned in this section can increase agility, enhance productivity, and substantially improve processes. The considerations provided with each technology are just a partial list of many others you must give attention to if you were to adopt it.

Even though executives understand the benefits, the path to adopting the technologies can be daunting. To be successful and remain ahead of the race, most companies need to execute and innovate quickly. Complete transition to digital cannot happen overnight, and hybrid models are more likely to emerge and become popular only if the company is ready to fully embrace the next-generation IT solutions in order to get to the customers first and create new growth. The hybrid solution is the infrastructure that will provide speed, security, agility, and flexibility. It will promote new applications and provide the ability to face future challenges. In recent years, we have witnessed a boom of new technologies emerge (Figure 1.2).

1.6.1 Digital Design

In the field of graphic design, digital technology is used to manage and create visual designs of technical projects and develop strategies with electronic technology that focus on humanizing information and customer experience for the web as well as for television, print, and portable electronic devices. There are

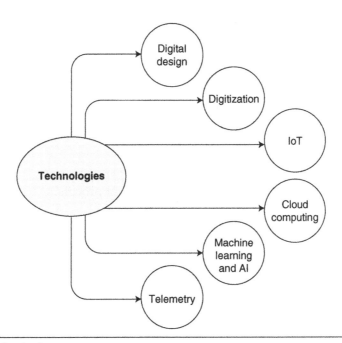

Figure 1.2 Technologies.

a number of benefits offered by digital design, including simplification of processes that used to be tedious and complex. The greatest benefit is that each layer of the design can be created and recreated until perfection is derived.

The digital designers are experts who create graphic design with skills and imagination to produce visual media by using three-dimensional (3D) graphic modeling, typography, screenwriting, video editing, video products, and motion graphics. The product is created from scratch with a target audience in mind and is accessed on a digital platform. The digital designs are first created to provide visual designs by using software programs that are readily available.

Digital design is also used to create prototypes of products, such as houses and consumer products. Designs are then socialized and refined based on continuous feedback, and new designs are created.

We would like to draw your attention to the terms *user interface (UI) designs* and *user experience (UX) designs*, which are often used synonymously for digital designs. In many companies, both UI and UX are created using digital technology.

As a digital designer, the more tools, skills, and knowledge you have, the more you can creatively contribute to interactive conversations with cross-functional stakeholders, including users. You will be able to direct the success of the project to encompass a variety of useful functionalities, design flows, and interfaces. To give you a sample of the job roles in digital design, here is a list that encompasses some of them:

- Web designer

- Artist for special effects

- Animation designer using 2D or 3D

- UI/UX designer

1.6.1.1 Digital Design Considerations

The widespread use of digital design shows that it is a powerful tool to increase efficiency. A few precautions must be taken:

- There must be sound processes and management practices to avoid any future problems in the product development process.

- Because the technology is easier to use and many computer-aided design (CAD) packages are inexpensive, digital design provides designers with an opportunity to frequently change the prototypes, which makes the design fluid; in turn the design may take longer to finalize and may take up more of the designer's time. Thus, it becomes a costly proposition to use digital design if the process is not controlled.

- The draft of the design can be generated in a very short time; this may lead to valid concerns regarding an incomplete understanding of the user's needs.

- The traditional designers take user requirements into consideration and spend time in understanding how the final product will be used. On the contrary, anyone who is computer savvy and has enough experience in computing is able to develop digital designs, with much less knowledge about the user.

1.6.2 Digitization

Digitization is a process of converting information in digital format. The word *digital* describes electronic technology that generates, stores, and processes data in a digital format that can be understood by computer systems, and digitization is used by a number of consumer electronic devices. To meet customer requirements, present and future, requires businesses to be customer oriented, efficient, and well connected. For optimization of business processes and procedures, digital transformation is a road to having robust, enterprise-wide strategies to achieve success in meeting customer expectations and, ultimately, to have a sustained, effective, and prosperous business.

Even though there appears to be a wide interpretation of the term "digitization," in our opinion, it is a process of transfiguring offline business processes into computer-supported and network-capable ones where the data can be accessed by anyone. For example, if a file is stored in the cloud, it can be accessed and viewed by anyone who has access to it. Therefore, to increase productivity, businesses digitize their processes and information so they can be accessed in seconds by employees worldwide. As opposed to storing information on paper in cabinets or drawers, digitization also helps to preserve critical information in a way that does not fade or become damaged over time.

1.6.2.1 Digitization Considerations

The main purpose of digitization is to collect data, analyze and implement the necessary processes to help the customers stay competitive, and remain relevant in the digital era. Focus should be placed on the following:

- Readiness of your company for digitization—that is, support from leaders and training for the employees.

- Employee awareness of the problems you are trying to solve. If there is no deep understanding, chances are employees will go along because they are mandated to do so; however, when it comes to adherence, those employees will be the first to deviate.

- Enhanced communication with the employees to ensure the best way to stay knowledgeable. You may want to set up networking sessions with subject matter experts to share experiences and set up knowledge-sharing sites.

- The effect of digitization on everyone, including your partners and suppliers in communication meetings.

- Planning for data collection, storage, and analytics.

- Consideration of how the data will be used and how associated measures of success will be implemented. Think through the fact that digitization takes different metrics than what you may have already established.

1.6.3 Internet of Things

The Internet of Things (IoT) is growing rapidly. Year after year, more than 5 billion connected devices are shipped to users. This number is going to rapidly increase. Looking at devices such as Apple Watch or Fitbit, you can see how the physical fitness industry is affecting our lives with IoT. When it comes to health-related devices, however, adoption will not become major unless there is a dramatic increase in functionality.

In the connected world, it is interesting to see how software and hardware are used to monitor our daily lives. One example is Gatorade's use of a smart bottle (hardware) with a sweat patch that will connect to a mobile application (software) to monitor the hydration level of a person.

Why are we hearing so much about IoT? IoT has other names such as "Industrial Internet" or "Industry 4.0," which actually started with Germany's smart factories and includes components of IoT. IoT is a concept of connecting everything—coffee makers, washing machines, headphones, lamps, wearable devices, cars, refrigerators, dishwashers, radios, televisions, and many other things—to the internet, and also to other devices, with an on/off switch that is extremely efficient and appealing in today's lifestyle where everyone seems to be constantly "on the go." The connections can be people to people (p2p), things to things (t2t), and people to things (p2t). Gartner analysts have predicted that by 2020, 30 billion mobile phones, tablets, computers, wearable technology devices, and other types of connected devices will be in use.[2] In comparison, in 2009, there were only 2.5 billion connected devices in use, and they consisted primarily of mobile phones, tablets, and PCs. As a result, IoT will add $1.9 trillion to the economy as information technology (IT) spending continues to grow.

You may wonder why you would want all these connections. Let's take an example of p2t. If you are on your way home from work and stuck in traffic, with p2t you will be able to start your oven from the car and get it warmed up; then, when you arrive home, all you have to do is to put a frozen dinner in and not have to wait for the oven to warm up, saving approximately 10 minutes. Here is a second example. You loaded the dishwasher with dirty dishes last night but forgot to switch it on; you remembered this when you were at the office the next morning. With a p2t connection, you will be able to switch the dishwasher on from the office and have clean dishes when you arrive home. You do not have to wait until you get home again and thus are able to have a timely dinner on clean dishes with less frustration and more time to do other things.

"The traditional IT market is not going to grow at a faster rate anytime soon, if ever—increased growth will come from the nontraditional IT market," said Peter Sondergaard, senior vice president at Gartner and global head of research. "While in 2015, the combined IT and telecom market will hit nearly $4 trillion, the incremental revenue generated by the Internet of Things' suppliers is estimated to reach $309 billion per year by 2020."[3]

In general, businesses will be able to operate efficiently, with increased productivity, and we will see more startups with state-of-art technologies to make day-to-day life simpler and easier to manage.

1.6.3.1 *IoT Considerations*

With every connected device we own—including smartphones, tablets, home security systems, connected appliances, monitoring systems, and more—there are a number of elements that require our attention:

- *Security.* This is on top of everyone's minds as hackers become more proficient in accessing data and as personal identities are put at risk, along with personal and organizational data. Great care must be taken to ensure that only authorized users can access any data from any internet-connected device.

- *Scalable platform.* Strategic planning on the infrastructure and platform supporting all the devices is the number-one criterion for the success of IoT. When planning, the infrastructure and platform should support not only current demand of all the connected devices, but should also take into consideration future expanding demands.

- *Software testing and quality assurance.* Over the years, efforts in software testing and quality assurance have become much smarter. We now have requirements traceability, test plans, test cases, and input/output validations. However, with connected devices, the software has become much more complex and requires special attention in testing. New code or fixes for software that break old functionalities that were once working is becoming a common tale. With connected devices, a software glitch may have terrible consequences if a monitoring system is disabled.

  Developing a reliable software testing process is essential, especially in the case of IoT. Attention must be paid to third-party acquired code (outsourced) to avoid any future vulnerability.

- *Efficient support on usability interfaces.* Multiple connectivity may result in new problems and additional calls for customer support. Detailed attention on user interfaces and usability will help avoid multiple calls to support center personnel and decrease their workload.

- *Data collection and analysis.* In-depth planning is required for the type of data you want to collect from the vast, connected infrastructure of IoT. Collection is one issue, but who should be allowed to see that data and what are the plans to act upon the derived data is a whole new ballgame. Data for the sake of collection becomes a useless effort. Activities that are planned based on the data to improve customer experience and satisfaction is another story.

- *Industry and regulatory requirements.* There are different legal rules, standards, and policies related to data. You must make sure that you know the legal requirements and are in compliance with it.

1.6.4 Cloud Computing

Cloud computing is known as remote computing, where your data is stored somewhere remotely and can be accessed any time, but there is no need for a physical location in which to store the data. Another vendor maintains the data at a remote site, with privileges to access, update, and use it, for which the vendor is paid a fee. You own the data, but another vendor maintains it for you "in the cloud."

Network performance plays a huge role in the performance of cloud computing. By paying special attention to public and private cloud applications and cloud access versus intracloud networking, you will be able to better understand the implications.

There are several benefits of cloud services:

- It reduces cost by eliminating the need for IT resources, including hardware and software. You also do not have to worry about storing data and having several databases requiring maintenance and physical space. Subscribing to cloud services reduces the need for data storage capacity planning and crunching of related numbers.

- Data backup and recovery are much more efficient in cloud services because data can be reflected at several locations on the cloud provider's network.

- Productivity also increases due to elimination of the need to configure and maintain the hardware and software.

- There is an increase in performance as big cloud service vendors run on global datacenter networks, which drastically outperforms a single company trying to upgrade to the latest fast-running hardware.

Your company will have to engage differently with cloud providers because it is a cultural change in the way we work, collaborate with partners, and train employees. A complete change involves empowering employees, optimizing business processes, and reimagining how customer support and employees work with customers and adhere to processes.

1.6.4.1 Cloud Computing Considerations

That data is yours: you can access the files any time, you can update them any time, you can delete them any time, but someone else controls and protects the data. This mandates a necessity for you to start preparing for consistent configurations and monitoring:

- Standardize service-level agreements and security. If there are any security or regulatory constraints, ensure that the cloud vendor supports them.

- Systemize cloud compliance policies.

- Licensing can cost thousands of dollars and keep on increasing. Learn the details of the cost structure, and navigate through the "fine lines" so you are able to negotiate an amicable agreement.

- Study and know how your users access their data currently and how the cloud will change user experience. To access, will there be any additional entries required by the users?

- When something goes wrong, how efficiently will the cloud provider resolve the issue? This often becomes difficult when there is finger pointing and blame is shifted from one party to another. However, a clean licensing agreement outlining the intricate specifics will save headaches at a later time.

- From the onset of signing a license with a cloud vendor, start discussions on data backups, data recovery, data protection, and data corruptions. Look into how the cloud vendor addresses these significant issues.

We will discuss private versus public clouds further in Chapter 2.

1.6.5 Machine Learning and Artificial Intelligence

Computers have helped all of us and can outperform humans in calculations and counting; however, we cannot say that computers are "intelligent" machines because they are not able to do anything unless we have written programs for them to do specific tasks. The approach of writing programs allows the computer to learn from data without full comprehensive commands given by a programmer.

Machine learning is sort of *artificial intelligence (AI)* allowing applications to give accurate results without explicit programming. It is concerned with the design and development of algorithms that allow computer behavior to evolve based on empirical data. Algorithms are either a set of rules or processes used by a computer to perform calculation, data processing, and automated reasoning tasks. As the quantity of data generated from machines and applications grows exponentially, our ability to process the data manually to look for patterns and predict potential events is inversely proportional. The algorithms save time, increase productivity, allow receipt of the inputs, and predict outputs based on statistical analysis. The success of machine learning depends on the algorithms that control the search to find and build knowledge structures that can also problem solve, plan, or perceive.

The ability to program machines and software to learn from data patterns by either teaching them to respond to certain data patterns or allowing them to self-learn using feedback loops, by writing algorithms for the machines to provide needed information, has helped to expedite many business decisions.

In addition to other benefits, machines with programmed algorithms also allow us to process large amounts of unstructured data and predict outcomes using the patterns observed in the data. This process uses various algorithms and iterative processing to achieve the ability of prediction. For example, in

a particular piece of hardware, if the baseline is always 80% of CPU utilization and the probability of system instability goes up directly from this point,
then machine learning can predict the chance of failure when the CPU usage
reaches 98% based on previous baseline data.

In short, machine learning is teaching computers to learn as humans do.
One example is interpreting the data that are around us and using our intelligence
to classify those data. Due to the large amount of data available, increased
efficiency in algorithms, and increased computer power, machine learning is
leading-edge artificial intelligence, which is becoming a "norm" in large enterprises due to many benefits through this technology:

- Companies are able to develop the systems that are difficult, costly, and
  resource intensive if created manually because they require special skills or
  knowledge

- Data mining and analysis from large volumes of data can be done more
  efficiently, with accuracy

- Certain tedious tasks done by the humans that require some intelligence
  can be replaced by machines

Some machine learning algorithms in use today are:

- *Linear regression.* This predicts the value of something by establishing
  the relationship of variables it is dependent on and some kind of a linear
  dependency.

- *Logistic regression.* The algorithm predicts the probability of an occurrence
  of an event based on independent variables.

- *Decision tree.* This algorithm is used for classification of large data sets into
  two or more homogenous blocks. Further processing will result in things
  like propensity to do something.

- *K-nearest neighbors.* This algorithm is used for classification or regression
  by using the closeness of a given sample to the object that is either being
  classified or value predicted. It is extremely fast and the results easily
  interpreted.

- *Random forest.* This is an algorithm based on multiple decision trees
  wherein an object that needs to be classified or calculated is processed by
  the decision tree and the forest chooses the classification with most votes.

- *Naïve Bayes.* This is an algorithm based on Bayes's theorem and is
  mostly used for text classification. It assumes features in a class are
  completely independent of other features in a class and, as a result, it can
  be extremely fast because multiple independent threads can be run to
  calculate the probability.

The concepts of machine learning, cheaper data storage, powerful computers,
and new capabilities acquired by data scientists are making it possible for

deep learning so that the new technologies can be used to do many of the tasks that seemed impossible just 20 years ago; a perfect example is a driverless car. Machine learning allows development of models to solve a given problem.

1.6.5.1 *Machine Learning and Artificial Intelligence Considerations*

Because machine learning uses algorithms to help computers do things that are done by humans and are, in many cases, tedious, efforts must be made to concentrate on challenges surrounding the technology:

- Large amounts of raw data in a storage repository is commonly known as a *data lake*. This raw data can be analyzed by machine learning, thus increasing demand for more data.

- The data lakes have the following risks: oversharing information; increasing loss of privacy; and disseminating the data unintentionally into the wrong hands, which may result in legal implications.

- In machine learning, the accuracy of the algorithm is based on the data it trains on. Therefore, if the data is unreliable, the algorithm will be negatively affected, and the results will be corrupt.

1.7 TELEMETRY

Telemetry is an automatic way of collecting data at remote sites or locations and transmitting the data to collectors at the receiving equipment for monitoring, analyzing, and taking appropriate actions based on the insights provided by the data analytics. Chapter 2 will delve further into this topic to provide you with more complete details, along with the associated benefits, and will use cases to help you organize the data to empower customers to use your products efficiently.

1.8 DISRUPTIONS DUE TO DIGITAL TRENDS

As digital transformation reshapes business models and businesses, strategic planning, careful collaboration, and ongoing attention from your executives will be needed to constantly monitor industry trends and the impact of digital technology on your company since these disruptions also have major impact on the resources (see Figure 1.3).

The rapid advancement of the technologies we described earlier and others is the foremost cause of digitization and globalization, which promote customer care and create new business models that can be introduced at a lightning pace with declining costs. Many of these digital disruptions are driving changes, which in turn generate data that can be used to improve customer experience, both at the local level, responding to the customer and paying attention to

Figure 1.3 Disruptions affect resources.

interactions with the customers, and at a strategic level, where information is integrated from various sensors to capture trends such as:

- *Shared rating.* The shared rating introduced by Uber used by both the drivers and passengers is now also used by other industries—for example, by hotel industries to rate the guests. Uber has also disrupted the market by bringing together drivers and passengers (sellers and buyers) in return for a transaction with zero marginal cost, which is a huge benefit.

- *Social media.* Fashion designers are able to connect to consumers directly through the use of social media. Designers such as Tommy Hilfiger and Burberry have announced that they will be able to ship their footwear immediately, thereby getting rid of the old method where buyers from retail companies reached out to these designers and negotiated merchandise deliveries and potential customers had to wait for months until the shops were stocked with that merchandise.

- *Shopping centers and stores.* We already have seen a rapid decline in the foot traffic in many of the stores and malls across America. "Cyber Monday" has become an acceptable practice, with millions of consumers purchasing goods online during the holidays. This has contributed to increased business and revenue for shipping companies such as UPS and Federal Express.

  The demand for large stores will be reduced and the need for huge inventories will diminish slowly as internet buyers become savvier, comparing prices and getting into money-saving efficiency patterns. This phenomenon will affect store loyalty, which will slowly become a thing of the past.

- *Non-auto owners.* With Uber providing easy and hassle-free access to transportation, along with companies such as Lyft, owning an automobile will become less frequent. Car2Go has disrupted the market by providing temporary access to products and services available traditionally only by purchasing them. Millennials have already shown that they care less about possessing things and more about a carefree life, with no insurance or auto maintenance hassles. When transportation is available on an as-needed basis, many are deciding against owning a car and being bogged down with associated repairs and upkeep—not to mention deciding against paying thousands of dollars upfront to purchase a vehicle, only to find that the minute it leaves the dealer, it has lost value and starts depreciating.

- *The subscription model.* With the Software as a Service (SaaS) or As a Service (aaS) subscription model, the traditional method of selling the product/service with a one-time payment will slowly disappear, and consumers will be charged an ongoing fee for continued access to the software. Apple Music, Netflix, and others have disrupted the market by taking a product that is usually purchased and securing repeat customers on a subscription-based model.

- *Self-driving cars.* It is not just Google that is investing in autonomous-vehicle R&D; most car manufacturers are developing prototypes. Safety is still a concern, but the idea of a self-driving car is still very much at the forefront of the automotive industry's research efforts. Fast forward 15 years, and you will see greater numbers of reliable self-driving cars, special highways, and an aging population with more freedom to move around easily.

With today's mantra of disrupt or be disrupted, these examples are just a few of several hundred thousand disruptions that are forcing organizations to look beyond the present business universe as they know it and start rethinking how things can change to capture the market share and retain their customer base. It is fair to say that robots are not on their way to taking over many of the jobs—they are already here! They will be coworkers in many factories and businesses. With artificial intelligence, the increase in the number of social robots that can talk and read sentiments are going to be on the rise, and these will be used as digital assistants. We will start trusting robots more, to the extent that it will not be just blue-collar jobs being lost to robots, but also white-collar jobs.

Regardless of the business sector and functional organization you work in—such as sales, marketing, customer support, or R&D—you will need to stay abreast of potential disruptive digital technologies. These will no longer affect just the leaders of businesses, but will affect individual contributors, middle managers, and senior managers as well.

In addition to the technologies that enable you to positively affect your customer experience and expectations, results of continuous improvements within your company also have a huge impact on company credibility and brand.

1.9 CONTINUOUS IMPROVEMENT

Continuous improvement seems to be a buzzword we hear often. The term seems to be simple, but how do you identify areas of improvement? The standard Plan, Do, Check, and Act (PDCA) cycle does not address the complexities involved. Continuous improvements have to go beyond posters that are stuck in conference rooms and office lobbies and has to become a way of life for all employees. Better yet, it has to become muscle memory for each and every employee. Continuous improvement ranges from small improvement opportunities to a large, companywide focus to reduce customer churn and increase revenue. It is a differentiation that helps attract new customers and retain the current base.

1.9.1 Why Is Continuous Improvement Important?

The question is simple; however, there is a lot of depth to it. It is very similar to ask, "Why is it important to eat healthy food?" Let's look at it: if you eat junk food, chances are you will be overweight, have high blood pressure, possibly have diabetes, and may not be able to enjoy life to a full extent. The list can go on. In the same way, if your company does not emphasize continuous improvement, there are drastic consequences. Let's explore a few of the rationales:

- These days, consumers are connected to information and news everywhere through the internet. With Twitter and Facebook, we do not have to look elsewhere to find information on a product or a company. Word of mouth is the most effective marketing tool. If you are continually improving your products, the market is going to react swiftly, and the flow of information will quickly reach potential buyers.

- Because of data and information accessibility, consumers are becoming smarter and know what their options are when selecting products. They not only look at the cost of goods, but also review quality and functionalities as well. If your product is similar to everyone else's, how will it stand out, and how will it attract a buyer's attention? Stagnant products with little or no innovation will die a slow death because consumers now have more options to buy what they need when they need it. You now need to worry about global as well as local competition.

- Improvement ideas literally come from everyone within a company. If there are organizational processes to evaluate these ideas and then implement the top 10% to 15%, depending on the idea, product development, customer support, or other functional organizations can be more efficient, thus saving hundreds of dollars and better utilizing resources. If there is no process to evaluate new ideas, the products will become stale and cease to attract customers.

- Continuous improvement promotes a highly agile working environment, where there is frequent knowledge sharing, collaboration, and teamwork that can lead to a quantum leap in customer satisfaction, productivity, or revenue.

- Your chances of radically innovating something new, bringing it to the market, and capturing a larger share of the market—but also gaining a reputation as a market leader—are greatly increased.

Continuous improvements cannot be successful without focusing on consistent corrective and preventive activities, as well as focusing on the time you take to address any customer-related issues and correct and prevent them from happening again. These two steps are necessary to gain customer confidence in products you offer.

1.10 PROACTIVE VERSUS CORRECTIVE VERSUS PREVENTIVE IMPROVEMENTS

1.10.1 Proactive Improvements

To be proactive, you have to plan and implement corrective actions before something is broken. Continuous improvement must be part of your business model to gain visibility into opportunities that need to be addressed for enhancements. Reviewing patterns of customer complaints and issues arising from malfunctioning products should be an awakening of corrective as well as proactive actions. Systematically adhering to an approach to identify and prioritize improvement opportunities, analyzing each, reviewing the impact and end results, and finally developing a solution will support staying abreast of many creeping problems at a later time.

Understanding customer complaints, returned products, and what your customers are saying about your products on social media and then analyzing these collective data will consistently provide reliable evidence to enable you to move forward in designing practical tactics for advancement in applying proactive actions prior to any potential issues. This is known as a *leading indicator*—that is, something you still have ability to influence positively by additional process corrections, additional testing, or additional reviews.

Corrective and preventive actions (CAPAs) are steps taken by your company to address and eliminate causes of nonconformities.

1.10.2 Corrective Improvement

Very simply, corrective improvement is an action that deals with a nonconformity that has occurred. The words *corrective improvement* suggest a lagging indicator, where something unwanted or derogative has already happened; exists now and must be fixed; and, at the same time, requires action to stop it from happening again. For example, if you released a software product that had defects encountered by your customers, complaints will start coming in, and you will assign someone to address those complaints. The engineer assigned will have to correct the code, test it, and send it to the customer—but now, you also have to implement process to ensure the problem does not occur again.

Correcting a problem is not as simple as it seems. The defect is now corrected, but you will have to manage customer communication to guarantee customer relations are maintained and the customer will continue to do business with you as a repeat customer. If the defect was major and had a vast negative impact on the customer's business, you will have to not only pacify the customer, but also ensure the story of the defect does not hit newspaper headlines, which will create a massive workload for your communications and brand management divisions. The workload increase will translate into hundreds of man-hours, equaling lots of revenue lost.

You may have corrected the problem reported by the customer; however, chances are you have not made the customer happy because the problem was already encountered and the customer had to spend time contacting you, letting you know about the problem, and then waiting for the fix to arrive. The damage of customer dissatisfaction is already done. We have seen companies where "time to fix a problem" is monitored, and engineers who speed up the process of providing fixes are rewarded. In our opinion, this encourages negative behavior. The emphasis and reward should be given to doing the things right the first time and not for corrective actions.

1.10.3 Preventive Improvement

A preventive action is one that prevents potential problems from occurring in the first place. The preventive action emphasizes the opportunity to isolate potential issues and proactively address them before they become major incidents. The difference between corrective and preventive improvement can also be addressed by two simple questions: Corrective—what action has been taken to correct the problem? Preventive—what change could be implemented to fix or address a weakness in the process (where the risks are high that there will be a defect) that has not yet caused any problem but that could, if not addressed? Preventive action also commonly includes improvement steps that result in increased efficiency, productivity, or cost reductions or provide other beneficial outcomes. When preventive actions are required, the following steps are adhered to:

- Action plans are developed with inputs from stakeholders

- Plans are reviewed for additional feedback

- Implementation of the plan takes place, and affected employees are trained

- Monitoring and measurement are done to ensure the implementation plan is working positively and to confirm preventive actions are effective

- Adherence to the plan is monitored to avoid deviations

- Employees are retrained on an as-needed basis

By concentrating on preventing problems early, you will be able to stop the issues from happening and will encounter significantly less costs than fixing them later.

For preventive improvement, the question is what has been done to ensure the problem is identified at the root cause and fixed so it does not happen again. Root cause analysis is a popular tool to identify the initial cause of an issue, address the opportunities for improvement, and stop recurrence of a similar failure or breakdown.

1.10.4 Root Cause Analysis

The process of *root cause analysis (RCA)* is to identify the fundamental and under-lying reason an issue occurred; it identifies one or more process failures that need correction. Fixing the identified causes will allow you to fix systemic problems. The process of RCA requires considering all the possible "what," "why," and "how" questions to discover the root cause(s) of an incident. For example:

- Why did a software defect escape?
- Was the software code tested?
- Was there adequate time allowed for the system testing?
- Was the engineer who developed the code given adequate time to write the code and conduct appropriate tests?
- Was a code review conducted?
- Was there adequate coverage in the testing?
- If adequate time was given for testing and code review, then why did the defect still escape?
- Did the engineer who performed the test have any formal training?
- Was a system test plan written, reviewed, and approved?
- Was all the feedback received from the review incorporated in the test plan?
- Were regression tests conducted?

Answers to all the questions with "whys" and "whats" will ultimately lead you to one or more reasons that contributed to the ultimate defect. The practice of RCA attempts to isolate, as much as possible, the failure occurrence.

1.10.4.1 Root Cause Analysis Tools

There are several popular RCA tools. To get the right results, you may want to utilize a combination of these tools rather than relying on just one of them:

- Checklists
- Brainstorming
- One-on-one interviews for data gathering
- Cause-and-effect identification
- Timelines

Checklists and brainstorming can be used for simple issues. For more complex issues, you may want to use cause-and-effect identification or logic/event trees, which are often supported by timelines. One-on-one interviews will provide additional (and broad) information as well as different perspectives on what may have caused the problem. However, determining the root cause in a large project involving multiple resources is difficult because you have to interview and collect data from a seemingly endless string of people, evaluate the processes, and possibly go through thousands of data sets to isolate the right issues. When it comes to data, it is clear that in order to ensure productive RCA, good, reliable data need to be in place, and this necessitates creation of common standards for retrieval and analysis of the data.

Regardless of the tool used, there are fundamental questions for which the answers must be obtained to have success in the RCA process:

- Why did it happen?

- How did it happen?

- What must be addressed to correct the problem?

1.10.5 Five Whys

The Five Whys is an RCA technique that can be used in the analyze phase of the Six Sigma DMAIC (define, measure, analyze, improve, and control) process. In comparison with other RCA tools, this technique promotes identification of many causes.

By asking "why" five times, you are able to peel away and identify layers of symptoms, which should ultimately lead you to the most likely problem. In complex cases, you may have to use the "why" a few additional times to narrow down the actual cause(s). It is one of the simplest tools to use and just requires discipline to determine the relationship between different causes of the problem.

The simple way to use Five Whys is to document the problem, ask "why" five times, and document the answers. Depending on who was involved in the project and where the issue occurred, for each "why," you may have to interview cross-functional people, or you may need to talk to individuals from different departments.

1.10.6 Cause and Effect

The cause-and-effect tool is also known as a fishbone diagram, Ishikawa diagram, or herringbone diagram. The diagram was developed by Kaotu Ishikawa, and it is a method of identifying all root causes that potentially contribute to an effect. It is used when you are trying to identify possible causes of a breakdown or a failure. The completed diagram resembles a skeleton of a fish, hence the words *fishbone* and *herringbone* used to describe it. The tool is extremely popular in industry because there is very little training required.

1.10.6.1 Steps for Cause and Effect

1. Agree on a problem and write it down on the left center side of a white board and draw a box around it.

2. Draw a straight horizontal line going to the box.

3. Brainstorm all the causes and list them on different branches coming out of the original horizontal line. Capture similar topics on the same branch and give a high-level topic name to each branch. Draw a box around each of these topics.

4. By asking "why," you will be able to drill down deeper into the causes of each branch, which must also be documented.

5. Once all the causes are identified, the ideal process will be to review each cause and determine the top five that contributed the most toward the original problem. The rationale is that not all causes are equal, and you will not be able to address every cause due to time and resource constraints.

6. Take the five top causes and for each, identify the ideal process to eliminate the cause and document it.

7. At the end of this exercise, you will have five separate processes.

8. Review each process with the stakeholders to obtain their inputs and buy-in. Update based on the feedback.

9. Develop and provide training for functional groups that will be affected by the new or changed processes.

10. Measure the success of each process.

11. Establish a governance structure to ensure continuity and success of the enhanced process. Hold individuals accountable for deviations to the preestablished process.

Figure 1.4 is an example of a competed cause-and-effect diagram.

1.11 CHANGE MANAGEMENT

The colossal roadblock to the success of continuous improvement is change management. Because most people resist change, it becomes hard to implement continuous improvement, which may require a complete new way of addressing a business activity.

If employees do not understand why the change is made, it will be hard to get buy-in. They will feel that the change is forced upon them, and you may lose valuable resources and knowledge that are difficult to replace. It has to be considered that it is hard for just about everyone to change, and if the change is not implemented the right way, it can turn out to be expensive and a

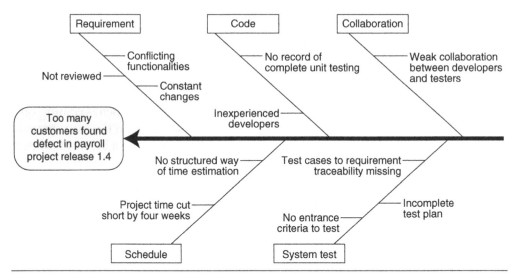

Figure 1.4   Example of a cause and effect diagram.

Figure 1.5   Forces of change.

failed attempt. Success depends on being aware of the art of change management and the entire cycle of change implementation, including reasons, types, stages, phases, and forces that may be against accepting the changes.

1.11.1 Reasons for Implementing Change

There are many reasons a change may be needed, such as business needs, keeping up with the competition, the worldwide environment, and technology. We have discussed many of these elements before. Change is also implemented due to threats, fraud, security etc. (see Figure 1.5).

1.11.2 Types of Change

Even though change is a constant in our lives, very few of us understand the different categories of it. Planning and implementation depend on the type of change you are going to pursue:

- *Anticipatory change.* Where a change is implemented with prior anticipation of the happening of an event. For example, if the public is aware that the taxes are going up 2% for the following year, they will anticipate this change for the next year.

- *Directional change.* Becomes necessary due to increasing competitive pressures or rapid changes in governmental control or policies. We have often seen that foreign goods cost more than the ones manufactured or produced locally, even though the functionalities may be the same. This is certainly directional change in price setting to discourage citizens from buying items that are competing with local goods.

- *Strategic change.* May affect different parts of an organization and also the organizational strategy—for example, change in the management style in an organization. It is structured and rolled out in a thoughtful way to meet the organization's goals, mission, and purpose.

- *Planned change.* It is implemented with the objective of improving the present method of operation to achieve the predefined goals.

- *Incremental change.* Small changes that will eventually result in a larger change that will have positive effects. The idea is not to disrupt everyone with one huge change, especially if there is a push-back from some. It is easier for individuals to accept small changes, and before they realize it, the small changes add up and a become large transformation.

1.11.3 Stages of Change

The process aimed at helping employees understand, accept, and adopt organizational changes and managing the transition becomes easier if it is done in five stages:

1. *Awareness.* All employees at every level are made aware that a change is coming and given time to prepare themselves mentally

2. *Desire.* The majority of the employees are convinced that the change will be beneficial and advantageous for the overall company

3. *Knowledge.* Employees understand the reason for the change and the actual benefits the change will bring

4. *Ability.* Each individual is trained for the change and given adequate tools to operate successfully to embrace the change

5. *Reinforcement.* Employees are given the opportunity to provide input related to the change; when successful, various functional areas are acknowledged and their success and contributions are reinforced

1.11.4 Change Implementation Phases

Change management is a structured approach to move employees and the entire company from the current state to a desired future state. The approach can be applied when adding a new process, technology, or product; hiring a large number of employees; or downsizing. Employees need to buy into the change proposal and start using it as well as becoming advocates to convince others to use it, too.

The following sections outline three different phases and an associated high-level list of actions to pursue when implementing a change.

1.11.4.1 Preparation Phase

- Allocate resources

- Assess current knowledge baseline

- Assess tool required to implement the change

- Determine type of documentation that will be required such as process flow, cheat sheets, or instruction manual

1.11.4.2 Management Phase

- Provide training to all employees and, if needed, to partners and the supply chain. Also provide ongoing training. When training is provided infrequently, there is a tendency to forget. At the same time, the new employees should be cognizant of what is expected from them. Ongoing training is a refresher course for old employees and beneficial for new ones.

- Identify roles and responsibilities, especially when implementing a new process.

- Provide guidance as to who will be accountable for ensuring smooth adoption.

- Provide frequent communications to the employees, letting them know the ongoing status of the change.

- Remove roadblocks by breaking cross-departmental silos.

1.11.4.3 Sustaining Phase

- Acknowledge success. This is the single most powerful technique to encourage employees to continue to adhere to the change.

- A reward system is always helpful to let the employees know they are being appreciated for their extra efforts, especially when it is a difficult and complex technology they have to adopt or if the learning curve of the change is steep and will require a complete 180-degree change from the current process.

- Emphasize accountability. This is where leadership plays a large role. If a changed process is not being adhered to and no one is held accountable for it, the tendency to ignore the change will become widespread. The moment there is a deviation to the changed process, management must step in to stop it from spreading by holding individuals accountable for the nonconformity.

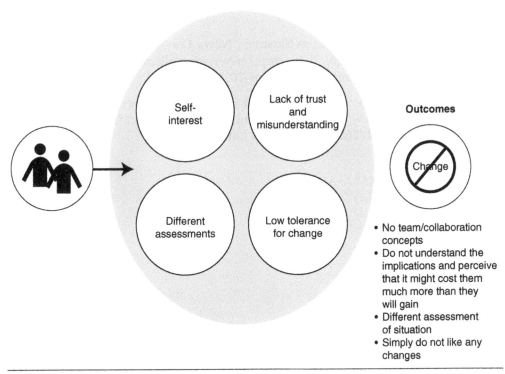

Figure 1.6   Forces against change.

* Ongoing monitoring is required to avoid departure from the newly implemented change and make sure that it is working as intended. Metrics and measurements on the success are a vital part of monitoring.

1.11.5 Forces against Change

Successful change management also involves identifying forces against adoption of change up front to manage these from the beginning. As shown in Figure 1.6, there may be a few employees who have self-interest at heart, while others may have a lack of trust and misunderstanding; some others may have made a completely different assessment of what the change is about and feel that it will be more costly; still others may simply have a low tolerance for a change. Address these individually to ensure a smooth transition.

Remember that without implementation of successful and results-oriented change, your business will likely fail to accomplish many needed innovative and quality improvements, resulting in the loss of competitive edge and a failure to positively affect customer satisfaction, which is the fundamental foundation for customer loyalty.

NOTES

1. Jeffrey Gottfried and Elisa Shearer, "News Use Across Social Media Platforms 2016," May 26, 2016, http://www.journalism.org/2016/05/26/news-use-across-social-media-platforms-2016 (accessed February 28, 2018).

2. "Gartner Says Personal Worlds and the Internet of Everything Are Colliding to Create New Markets," November 11, 2013, https://www.gartner.com/newsroom/id/2621015 (accessed January 17, 2018).

3. Ibid.

2

Telemetry Overview

In this chapter, we will provide detailed context of what telemetry is, what it accomplishes, and why it is needed.

Telemetry is product-specific data that is collected where the device or an application resides; the data is sent to a central collection point for ingestion and further processing. This data will be specific to the device and intended use but is valuable when designed into the product, with ultimate-use cases driving the device. Depending on the design, the telemetry data is sent back to the company to enable proactive actions in case of issues arising or functionality malfunctioning. With data available through telemetry and appropriate analytics performed, you can save on customer support costs because you have the capability to call the customer prior to receiving a call from him or her. In addition, you will be in a position to influence the customer's experience with your company. Without receiving advance data on the functionality of the products at the customer' site, the customer service center becomes the focal point for customer use.

2.1 CUSTOMER SERVICE

When a customer tries to use the product you sold and faces a problem, your customer service will be the first functional organization to hear from the customer. *Customer service* is the pre- or post-sales support you provide to a customer. The customer service process assists a customer in the use of your product by answering simple inquiries about the product and troubleshooting customer-encountered problems while using some of the product functionalities. Depending on the company, customer support employees may also train the customer to provide guidance in the implementation of latest upgrades. Many individuals work behind the scenes to address a problem reported by a customer; however, it is the customer support team that directly connects with the customers to understand the details of the problem. Because these employees are the first individuals to interact with customers, they are in a position to influence customer perception about your company, and they are in the best position to limit the churn of the customers by providing courteous and timely responses to solve problems. Let us walk you through a scenario where receiving information through telemetry can help enhance a customer's interaction with your company:

> Joe Blank is a payroll administrator in a company that has 5800 employees; the employees are paid on a biweekly basis. He is about to generate the payroll when the system suddenly stops. After a 30-minute, futile effort to revive the system, he calls your customer service department. By now, he is frustrated because he is running behind schedule and would like to move on to the next item he has to address. With telemetry, you are able to receive the data about the system stop when it happens and proactively provide the fix to Joe, before he calls you. Responding quickly and efficiently, you have now increased Joe's satisfaction. He will be willing to accept the fact that there was a defect in the payroll system but that it was solved in an efficient manner.
>
> On the contrary, if Joe Blank had to rely on the support representative to do the analysis after he reported the problem, extra time would have been required, resulting in a negative experience with the support representative and the company. The likelihood of Joe calling the support team again with a problem will be low. In addition, the possibility of him recommending your product to someone else will be less likely.

If customers dread calling to resolve issues, the brand damage to the company will be slow but steady. You want the support group to not only address the problems immediately with the results of analysis of the telemetry data, but also provide feedback to the rest of the organization based on the evaluation of the probe so that the data can be used to improve products and processes to stop similar issues arising in the future.

The medical industry has been using telemetry data to assist patients for several years. Cardiovascular diseases are one of the leading causes of deaths worldwide. For this reason, patients with heart conditions are monitored on an ongoing basis by an electrocardiogram (ECG) device that the patient wears. The device monitors and picks up the patient's heart activity and transmits the records of the rhythms in patterns that are then evaluated by technicians. Evaluation of the recording helps the cardiologist identify abnormalities and provide appropriate treatment. In this example, the telemetry data is collected when the device resides on the patient.

If there are no automated monitoring tools, the performance of your products becomes almost invisible and the data collected becomes questionable. You have to rely solely on patients to manually record discomforts they are feeling at a given time or for products in other sectors, have the customer complete the surveys or contact customer support, and report the difficulties—thus relying on a manual method to collect the data. There are several drawbacks to manually collected data:

- Duplicate or irrelevant data

- Critical data missed

- Insufficient data collected to make the right decisions

- Conflicting data collected

- Data collected with biased opinion

- Some of the data lost over time

- Data collected at the wrong time rather than when something happened

- Data collected during large intervals, thereby making the data useless

With the mediocre, average response rate of 13% on distributed customer surveys, it is hard to make constructive decisions, especially when certain populations of customers may not participate in the survey at all due to either physical limitations or the unwillingness to answer certain questions because of time constraints. Even if all your customers are willing to complete the survey, it is difficult to design questions that can be interpreted the same way due to differences in education, ethnicity, age, etc., thereby giving you data that will not yield better results for you or your customers, even if you were to redesign some of the processes to address customer concerns.

Without state-of-the-art mechanisms in place for data collection, it is difficult to accurately capture data. The digitalized method of capturing product and customer data avoids most of the common issues discussed earlier and helps in:

- Getting real-time data to facilitate fact-based decisions

- Understanding customer interaction with your products, such as functionality or outage

- Knowing feature consumption and usage by industry segment

- Monitoring performance

- Containing any threats or intrusions

- Getting visibility to downtime

Collection and analysis of data through carefully designed use cases will provide you with several insights. Insights are either understandings or awareness of product-related issues that will make you take actions to address the issues, improve a product, or contact the customer before he or she has a chance to pick up the phone to call for support. This is one of the places where telemetry plays a vital role in providing efficient, proactive customer service.

2.2 USE CASES

A *use case* is a software and system engineering term that describes various actions or steps defining the interaction between a role (actor) and a system to fulfill a particular outcome or a goal. The actor can be an external system or a human such as a program manager, manager, clerk, or other. The main purpose of a use case is to define who interacts with the system, what role they play, and what activities they address. Multiple paths can be taken by a user in a use case.

The high-level steps for designing use cases are as follows:

- Determine the users of the system.

- Identify each user's role.

- Establish goals associated with each role to support the system.

- Create use cases for all the goals by defining how a user will use the system. Indicate what happens if the system succeeds and also if it fails. If there are any preconditions, they must be specified. Identify any exceptions and what happens when any of the exceptions is encountered.

- Write normal course of events.

- For each step, explain the responses of the system to the actions initiated by the user.

2.3 SIMPLE END-TO-END TELEMETRY

We now introduce you to the components of a simple telemetry system. As you go through the remaining chapters of the text, additional components will be added to build a complex, end-to-end telemetry system. As shown in Figure 2.1, each of these components has a specific role in ensuring the overall success of telemetry.

2.3.1 Producers

To understand the "Producer" role, we need to understand private and public cloud, data centers, and big data.

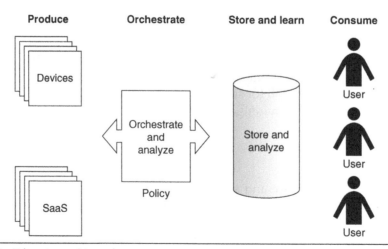

Figure 2.1   Telemetry end to end.

2.3.1.1 *Private Cloud*

A private cloud is dedicated to a single organization, where cloud computing resources are used by the organization that builds the infrastructure using its own servers and where those resources are managed and maintained by the company's own IT personnel. The private cloud can be located in the organization's onsite data center, and it delivers several advantages, including scalability and self-service, but through a proprietary architecture. The services and infrastructures are maintained on a private network.

The advantage of a private cloud infrastructure is that such structures are more secure because the servers on which the data reside cannot be accessed by other companies, and the data is more controlled. In addition, there are benefits such as improved up-time and reliability.

2.3.1.2 *Public Cloud*

Public clouds deliver services to multiple organizations and are operated and maintained by a third-party service provider using its own servers. The hardware and software related to a public cloud are owned and maintained by the cloud provider, who makes applications, data storage, and other resources available to multiple organizations. You subscribe to the services and manage your account using a web browser.

The shared computing environment of public clouds is not suitable for every business due to privacy, security, and up-time concerns. Before making a decision on whether to select a private or public cloud, your organization must consider several factors, including:

- How critical is your data?

- How secure do you want your data to be?

- Are there any regulatory requirements you need to adhere to?

- Are there any data protection laws you need to consider?

The examples of producer systems include IoT devices, hardware, software running on a private cloud, or software running on a public cloud. These devices have instrumentation built into them to capture events of relevance that can be used to drive use cases that are generally sent to a big data platform managed in a company's data center. In tandem with machine learning, described in Chapter 1, deep learning or just basic analytics is used to drive use cases.

2.3.1.3 *Data Centers*

A data center is a facility consisting of computers and storage of data where a company's IT operations and equipment reside. Data centers play a significant role in the continuity of the company's daily operations. To simplify the definition of data centers, we will say that it is a central location where computers and networking equipment reside for the purpose of collecting, processing, storing, and accessing a company's data that can be used to run day-to-day operations.

As the computers and servers became cheaper and our need for data grew, organizations started networking multiple servers to increase processing power. With communication networks, people can access the data remotely to analyze and utilize it for enhancing the overall business. With high-bandwidth broadband, internet, smartphones and other technologies, we are constantly demanding that more data be delivered on our phones, computers, and other devices.

Data centers use vast amounts of energy, and in some cases, the inefficient use of power is largely driven by the constant demand of employees to have the data at their fingertips, regardless of whether anything constructive is done with that data.

2.3.2 Orchestration/Policy Engines

This layer in the architecture generally is responsible for the onboarding of a device through standard handshakes like exchange of secure tokens and certificates. A *secure token* is generally a small device that authorizes a user to access network services, and it contains a password that is transmitted for each authentication. This type of device is not very secure; hence there are now synchronous dynamic password tokens where various password combinations are produced by an algorithm, which provides maximum security. The device can be in form of a fob or a small card. Many apartment buildings provide their residents with key fobs that allow them to enter the building; similarly, hundreds of companies give small identity cards to employees to provide access to the company's front doors.

Collecting data is not sufficient. We also must make sure that the data is valid, otherwise the analysis and decisions made based on the invalid data will cause further disruptions in customer satisfaction and overall product quality. Attention must be also given to guarantee that the data does not break any existing applications or systems. Invalid data can also be malicious and can cause complete system breakdown, which may then result in fraudulent activities. There are certificates that have a cryptographic key that, when installed on a server, is similar to a padlock and allows secure connections from a web server to a browser. Both tokens and certificates are functions absolutely necessary to reduce fraud and ensure only valid data is sent for processing. This component is generally used to run edge analytics (discussed next).

2.3.2.1 *Edge Analytics*

Instead of waiting for the data to be sent to a centralized data collection, when analysis of the data collected is done at a network switch, sensor, or some other device, it is known as *edge analytics*. In a traditional scenario, data is collected and sent to a data lake and analyzed at a later time. There are several disadvantages to this:

• By the time the data is analyzed, it may be too late or useless.

• The costs of collecting and storing the data can rise exorbitantly.

- Imagine the infrastructure required to collect the data and transfer it to a central location. As the demands of data increase, the load will double and triple in a very short time, creating a need to update the infrastructure often.

- If not planned properly, the massive amount of data in the lakes may become impossible to handle and the prioritization of what should be analyzed first will become next to impossible.

For these reasons, edge analytics is used when near-real-time events need to be processed to drive remediation and other activities back to the device/application sending the data. After real-time or post-event processing, when companies want to run analytics and drive actions based on such data, the policy engine in the "Orchestrate" layer can be used to drive actions to the devices or software by interpreting metrics, entitlements, and other relevant data. Orchestration engines generally run on the cloud and are also geographically distributed due to performance and security reasons. It is essential that these engines are built for cloud scale and are completely cloud enabled.

2.3.2.2 *Security Policy*

Having a security framework and a strong security standard is of utmost importance. Both you and your customer should know what security standards are in place and must be willing to participate in implementing them. Firewalls, malware software to prevent viruses, and employee training are necessary to protect your customers and your company from loss and thefts pertaining to identity. The larger scenario to worry about is the legal ramifications of such theft, and a security policy helps build customer trust and employee understanding of the established processes, procedures, and adherence required to keep your organization or system secure to prevent unintended access, virus attacks, and other activities that will cause issues with the day-to-day, smooth running of the company, including various IT systems.

Security is at the forefront of every business leader's mind and requires well-thought-out plans to minimize risks. Constant oversight and continuous vigorous communication are required to eliminate deviations of any process breach. It is similar to a switch: either you are fully secured or you are not secured at all. So establish the norms, taxonomy, procedures, and standards of security before even thinking of onboarding a customer.

2.3.3 Store and Learn

This layer consumes the data (real time or batch) presented by the orchestration layer and allows functions like basic analytics by grouping the relevant fields or advanced analytics using machine learning applications.

The store and learn layer stores information at scale and processes it by using iterative procedures, machine learning, and other technologies to drive insights such as predictions, pattern recognition, or propensity using algorithms in Python or R.

2.4 TECHNOLOGY SELECTION

You want to adopt a technology framework according to your business goals and one that has been tested and that works for other organizations. To successfully select and implement the right technology to match your company is a difficult task. There are a number of technology selection criteria, which should be data driven. Some of them are based on:

• Appropriate technology that will work for the type of business you are in

• Business objectives

• Needs of the customer

• Current knowledge of the employees who will have to work closely with the technology to achieve desired results

The challenge is that when the technology is adopted, it must be implemented successfully to derive the goals and benefits you are looking for. If you are incorporating third-party vendors (TPVs) into your products, you need to also consider if the technology selected will work with TPV products and if the TPV products are designed to capture the telemetry data. The more TPV products are incorporated with yours, the more challenging it is to adopt the right technology because integrating various components and platforms is not easy.

2.4.1 Users

The users utilize the analytics/insights to present information to stakeholders or create actions that will have to be addressed by relevant functions. Here are some examples of how various users take advantage of telemetry:

• *Engineering.* May build use cases based on product feature adoption, where the group uses feature usage data to understand which features are most often used by customers and which features are seldom used. As a result of this visibility, the following actions can be taken for the widely used features:
  — Allocate additional resources to continually enhance them
  — Spend more time in the design, development, and testing to ensure robust quality
  — Ensure support staff is adequately trained to provide detailed guidance on use
  — Strengthen marketing efforts
  — Create additional training materials
  — Develop most commonly asked questions/answers templates

  For features that are rarely used, engineering will be able to make data-driven decisions about whether to end those features or continue to provide minimum support.

• *Services.* May build applications for monitoring product quality; proactive issue detection falls under the category of "predictive telemetry," where services organizations can build analytics to understand which product has the greatest number of support/quality issues. The generated data can then be analyzed and used to drive improvement activities and increase product quality. Deep analytics will also provide insights on the devices exhibiting certain anomalies resulting in customer issues—for example, downtime. In this case, the awareness that downtime may occur can be used to drive a proactive replacement to make an update to the software to avoid system crashes and subsequent downtime before it even happens.

This scenario tends to strengthen customer relations because you are able to avoid a failure before it happens, and it saves both you and the customer hundreds of dollars and hours if the downtime had actually been encountered by the customer.

2.5 CONNECTED CUSTOMER EXPERIENCE

Telemetry is the only true way of seeing data that represents what the customer is experiencing at any point in time. As the industry moves to close monitoring of the systems—that is, "always on systems"—and insight-led actions in real time, the best way to ensure we are able to meet customer demand and also innovate with new offers is to thoughtfully include key events in software applications that interact with hardware, bring these events back to the company, and drive insights through large-scale, big data systems. The advantage with the store and forward architecture is that logic can be applied on the edge to take corrective actions at a local device/geography level. You do not have to wait until the data is processed and insights brought back from the central data processing engine.

The data is captured and iteratively processed. This provides different nuggets of information using data science at a later time, when additional time and resources are available. It also eliminates the necessity of getting services from costly consultants on an immediate-need basis.

2.6 MANUAL AND AUTOMATED DATA COLLECTION METHODS

In the past, companies used semi-manual and automated ways to get device and software data from the field. We discussed some of these methods in Section 1.2 of Chapter 1. Manual collection of data should be avoided because:

- Manual labor is not scalable

- It is error prone due to human intervention

- It is prohibitive due to costs involved

- Automation is essential in maintaining the integrity of data

- Faulty data increases risks associated with customers, businesses, employees, and the public in general

Telemetry now	Telemetry in the past
• No thoughtful instrumentation • Rigidity due to database design • High connectivity costs • High software cost for analytics at scale • Connected product use cases not prevalent	• Thoughtful events captured with use cases in mind • Schema-less database allows flexibility • Encrypted data on the internet provided at low cost with highly available connection • Open-source software provides cost-effective scale • Use cases explosion for using product data to drive intelligent action

Figure 2.2   Telemetry now and in the past.

Earlier automated methods of collecting and storing data in large-scale databases required dedicated connectivity, rigidity in design of the structures to store the data, extra resources to secure and handle the data, and additional expenses. Today's systems use encrypted data on the internet, big data open-source software, and schema-less design and offer unprecedented simplicity and cost advantages over earlier systems.

Figure 2.2 provides a quick view of past and current telemetry. Note that in the past, there was also low adoption of telemetry use cases except in mission-critical areas like communications satellite operations, defense, and other key areas. To elaborate on past data acquisition versus today, we need to understand the context of what was not available in the past and what makes it really relevant and easy today.

2.7 ABSENCE OF THOUGHTFUL INSTRUMENTATION

In the past, we saw that most companies were interested in releasing products in the market at the earliest possible time and did not bother about creating relevant code into the events at the time when the products would release. The consequence was that failure events and exceptions were captured after the fact. This created major issues because extra efforts were required in the analysis that had to be performed by subject matter experts (SMEs) who were not intimately familiar with the product. Many times, these SMEs were not involved in the design and development of the product and had very little knowledge of the process and the contents—that is, the features and functionalities.

With newer products hitting the market, this trend has been reversing as engineers and peripheral customer service functional departments have realized that product usage and exception data captured in real time give them immense power to influence customers' perceptions. They have also come to realize that data on usage of the product in the long run saves money because the knowledge will assist in improving the products further and will make them more efficient. In companies using agile methodology, many engineering teams are either engaged with or have ensured that telemetry use cases are tracked as separate user stories. The agile approach promotes speed and flexibility through collaborative cross-functional teams and focuses on delivery of individual functionality of an application to customers/end users. The user stories in these agile environments are consistently groomed and managed by product managers. The thoughtful orchestration of user stories also results in labeled data that can be used to rapidly train machine learning algorithms to drive immediate returns. This trend is definitely a win–win situation for customers and companies alike. The companies are able to get timely information to improve the product or to implement preventive measures before the customer is negatively affected. And the customer is able to continue business as normal, with no product issues.

2.8 RIGIDITY OF DATABASE DESIGN

Products tend to change from release to release, and the data captured or generated tends to change, too. In addition, as features are added or deprecated, new events are captured and new attributes are generated. In the world of databases, the schema or tables have to be carefully designed with number of fields, formats, dependencies, etc., and designed into the storage layer. If this was not totally rigid, the complexity of maintenance on a continual basis would not be an easy task and would cause significant costs to rework tables and ingest processes, analytics, and consumer applications. This causes low productivity and slow innovation. With the advent of schema-less or metadata-driven ingestion processes using big data applications, the procedure has become extremely easy and has caused an explosion in use cases, including telemetry.

Metadata refers to data that describes or provides additional information for other data, such as information about a title, subject, author, or size of a data file. It may also describe the accuracy, time, or date of the data that was acquired. For example, if you search on Google for a book, you use metadata; if you search for an article on birds, then you use metadata. IT systems are aided by metadata to find material users are searching for.

Generally, any changes to schema are easily ingested using metadata; the processing of the additional fields can happen after the fact, and new insights can be used to drive actions. The key takeaway here is that while schema-less/metadata-driven frameworks help with ingestion, storage, and analysis, work still needs to be done to either use the data in use cases or show it in a visualization layer. However, the work is significantly less and is faster.

2.9 HIGH CONNECTIVITY COSTS

As the explosion of connected hardware and software grows, the need for data pipelines to transport data grows exponentially. In the past, to connect the data securely, there was a need for dedicated connectivity such as T1 lines that were very costly and were operational headaches to maintain and manage. You may wonder what a "T1 line" is. A T1 line carries data at very high megabits per second or carries several digitized voice channels. Usually a phone company will use either a copper T1 line or a fiber-optic line in your company.

With the advent of encryption and secure virtual private networks (VPNs), the costs for transporting data have reduced considerably. Now it is easy for many small companies to create telemetry ingestion processes at a very reasonable cost, while securely transmitting the data over the internet using encryption, VPN, and other secure means. The cost reductions have also been passed down to customers, resulting in an upsurge of use cases where various devices (including IoT) can be switched on while continuously sending information back to the analyze engines.

2.10 HIGH SOFTWARE COST

Previously, the cost to ingest, store, and analyze large volumes of data was very high because the specialized software was expensive and required specialized hardware to run it. With open-source software that runs on generic and non-custom hardware, the cost to run the applications has significantly lessened (by many factors of 10). This savings has been reflected in the significant investments companies are making to focus on data processing and analysis to obtain insights. Where possible, analytical results are used to drive up profit margins through implementation of a product as well as by process activities that address innovation, improvements, and productivity and provide competitive advantages.

2.11 CONNECTED-PRODUCT USE CASES

The last and the most important area is the paucity of connected-product use cases, except in highly specialized use cases like SCADA (supervisory control and data acquisition), plant sensors, satellites, and the like. With availability of cheaper hardware like IoT sensors and also the volume of hardware/software that a company uses, the applicability of data from the above-mentioned devices to run use cases has exploded. This is an ideal situation because the preceding factors have created a need for an "always on" connected system with a low-cost insights engine.

2.11.1 SCADA

Supervisory control and data acquisition is a combined system of software and hardware that provides multiple facilities to organizations such as oil and gas, telecommunications, energy, and others. A SCADA system collects information on malfunctioning of a pipeline, alerts the main device of this event, and indicates whether it is critical. The main device may generate additional alerts to notify individuals who can fix the problem.

Here are some of the examples:

• Allows gathering, monitoring, and processing of real-time data

- Through human and machine interface, interacts with devices such as motors, sensors, and valves

- Creates log files with recorded events

2.12 RETURN ON INVESTMENT FOR TELEMETRY

With all the power over data comes great responsibility, too:

- Drive actions that benefit customers

- Provide outcomes in terms of reducing downtime

- Ensure high availability

- Secure the perimeters

- Influence the bottom financial figures while reducing costs

Here are some key examples we have seen where telemetry has provided immense value:

Use Case 1—Configuration Changes (Figure 2.3)

- *Device/application and telemetry capture.* The edge-connected security device or application constantly collects and pushes information about malware to the collector, which in turn collates and monitors the data.

- *Machine learning.* The device uses business rules generated by experts or machine learning, using elements like software version, signature version, and malware to understand what risks are inherent in the software, configuration, or any other data.

- *Actions.* The device uses either relevant configuration and software update or notifies the customer to address the inherent risks exhibited by the device or application.

Use Case 2 (Figure 2.4)

- Engineering teams constantly face a challenge understanding how product feature adoption is happening at a customer site and also which features are used by only a few customers or rarely used.

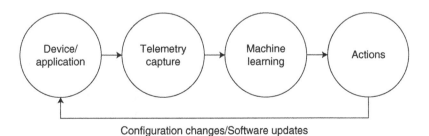

Figure 2.3 Telemetry use case 1 for configuration changes.

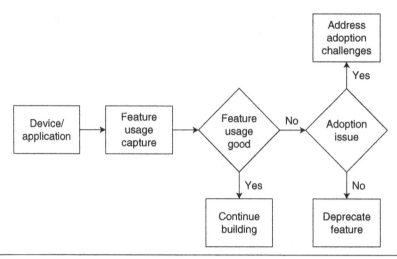

Figure 2.4   Telemetry use case 2 for feature adoption.

- By determining how much time a feature is used and by whom, engineering teams can understand what to do with the feature or help the customer adopt the feature, resulting in customer satisfaction.

- In cases where decisions are made to end low-performing product features, there is a huge cost savings that can be repurposed to build more adoptable features.

2.13 PREVENTIVE TELEMETRY

Previously, we provided a complete holistic picture of telemetry to expose you to the telemetry process and other logistics to enable you to grasp the deep concepts and new terminologies. Now we want to share examples of how telemetry is being used for preventive measures:

- *Healthcare.* Earlier in the chapter, we discussed how the medical industry is assisting patients in recording abnormalities of heart rhythms and proactively contacting them.

- *Software.* If the telemetry capability is designed in the software right from the beginning, it allows data related to functionality usage, product failure, or feature failure to be sent on a continuous basis to the company that developed the product. The data is automatically interpreted by intelligent software, and when there is a threat of a feature malfunctioning, the company is alerted. With the alert, the company can immediately assign engineers to work on the fix, test it, and push it to the customer, thus letting the customer know of a potential failure. By installing the fix immediately, the customer is able to address the problem before it really becomes a problem. The proactive service changes the customer support image perception to a very positive one.

If the preventive telemetry data was not available, the customer would have encountered a feature or total product failure, and this would have disrupted the customer's business and also negatively affected your company's quality image. Pushing the fixes proactively to the customer not only saves your company time and resources, but also does the same for your customer and helps build a solid relationship between the two parties. The customer feels cared for, and this certainly assists in creating positive brand impact.

The idea of preventive telemetry is to ensure your customers are on board with the concept of you collecting their data. Once you have gone through this hurdle, observing the functions used most by your customer, the functions where the customer has difficulties in use, or the functions that are about to fail becomes a breeze. Don't forget once the data is collected, corrective process must be put in place to avoid any incident from happening.

Preventive telemetry is a powerful concept because it helps to:

- Reduce support costs by eliminating the need for the customer to call.

- Reduce communication time because the problem is resolved up front, before it was encountered. Therefore, there are no phone calls or follow-up required.

- Eliminate the need for the senior management to get involved to pacify the customer. Because the customer was not affected by the failure of product functionality, he or she does not get a chance to get upset.

- Eliminate unnecessary media attention. Whenever there is a major problem encountered by a customer, the scenario catches media attention and, thus, negative publicity. But if the problem/issue is fixed, the media will not be involved.

For any customer information your company captures through the products you sell, the customers must be notified. Onboarding the customers on the idea that your company will be capturing information related to their usage and other pertinent data is not really appealing to many customers due to privacy and security concerns. In Chapter 5, we discuss this topic further.

Preventive telemetry can be used as one of the tools to stay ahead of the competition. Business indicators suggest that you need to keep an eye on your competitors because you do not want them to gain on you. Even if things are going great for you, if your products are continually enhanced and provide added value to your customers, and if your market share is growing, you still need to worry about the competition because all your customers may not be fully satisfied with your company. There is a certain percentage of dissatisfied customers in every field, and they may be ready to jump ship to another competitive vendor. If preventive telemetry is not used, chances are your customer will encounter issues, and with universal information sharing on social media, it is very easy for the word to travel. Such an information spread, especially if negative, may destroy potential future buyers' confidence in your company.

Telemetry can be used to design capabilities that ensure customer service is maintained through continuous monitoring of data from the devices and then comparing the data against a baseline of existing anomaly data and also against data from devices that are functioning normally. This is accomplished via machine learning by comparing key parameters from the device, such as CPU size, unhandled exceptions, system events, etc., and by using different algorithms to create predictive models.

The monetization opportunity exists here where the customer pays for a service level that allows for replacement devices to be shipped out with relevant configuration as soon as these failure conditions are encountered or predicted. The following use case further elaborates on this concept:

Use Case 3 (Figure 2.5)

- The edge-connected security device constantly collects pushes information about system stability to the collector, which compares the data with a baseline.

- Based on information of previous anomalies and outcomes checks, the customer is either sent a notice or scheduled for preventive maintenance; the customer may even schedule a device return material authorization (RMA).

2.13.1 Baselining of Data

Baselining is the initial collection of known data that is reviewed against subsequent unknown data for comparison or trending purposes. The activity of

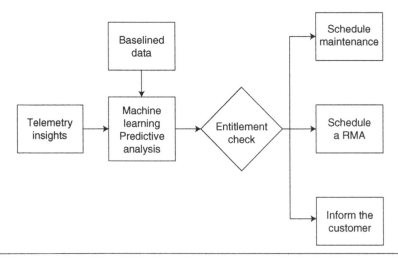

Figure 2.5   Using telemetry and entitlement to drive customer uptime/service level agreement.

capturing a baseline helps you to determine the normal working of the device and track changes. When baseline data is not available, it is difficult to:

- Know how the devices are working

- Estimate changes if the devices are not working in a normal way

- Compare the initial results to later results

Therefore, the activity of baselining must be given a priority in your telemetry project and must be one of the steps to address before starting the project. Often, baseline data is not collected due to:

- Insufficient planning and oversight

- Time constraints

- Resource constraints

- Evaluation not considered until late in a project

Devices behave differently in different configurations. The continuous baselining of data generated by a device working well is essential to ensure we understand the data patterns. Any exceptions to these patterns can be compared to other anomalies observed and the events that resulted from them.

The customer experience goes up dramatically if a customer is contacted ahead of time, prior to encountering the defect, and the likelihood of becoming a loyal customer, in this case, is much stronger. In addition, there is a large cost associated with customer-found defects—commonly known as "cost of poor quality" and poor product performance. Throughout the concepts of quality, the ultimate goal is to ensure smooth running of the functionalities of the product. But keep in mind that the ability to react swiftly will save the day, both for the customer and for your company.

2.14 COST OF POOR QUALITY

Even though in his famous book *Quality Is Free*, published in 1979, Phillip B. Crosby said quality is free, there is a cost associated with devising procedures to improve quality. We rarely pay attention to the cost of poor quality, especially when giving priority to time-to-market. Cost of poor quality (COPQ) looks at all the expenses associated with the activities you have to address once a problem is reported. IBM quality expert H. James Harrington made the concept of COPQ popular in his book *Poor Quality Costs*, published in 1987. In the process of calculating COPQ, you will generally collect the following data (see Figure 2.6):

- *Cost of labor to analyze the defect.* In order to fix the defect, it has to be appraised to find out the cause of the defect. Depending on the type of products you sell—such as hardware, service, or software—it may take one or more resources to comb through the sequence of events that led to the failure, review the components or the code, inspect the tests that were conducted, review the process that was adhered to, evaluate if there were any deviations to the preestablished process, and look at the accuracy of the test tools to make the determination of the failure.

- *Cost of labor for the rework to fix the problem.* Once the cause is identified, it has to be fixed. In the case of code, the new code has to be written and tested to ensure the original defect is fixed and the new code has not created any additional defects. The code needs to be sent to the customer, or it must be uploaded in a central place with customer notification to enable the download of the fixed code.

- *Cost of scrap and returned materials.* If the problem is a hardware product and is too cumbersome to fix, you may opt to scrap the returned material and issue new hardware.

- *Cost of lost opportunity.* The time it takes to address and fix various defects is really lost because you are engaged in rework and do not have time to innovate or pursue new opportunities to enhance the products or penetrate through to new marketing prospects.

- *Preventive action cost.* As a result of root cause analysis, you will be able to determine the finite reasons as to why a certain problem occurred. It is better to prevent defects in the first place than correct them. Remember that the majority of defects are preventable. To prevent similar incidents in the future, you will have to implement preventive activities, which may be related to:
  — Quality planning
  — A new process implementation

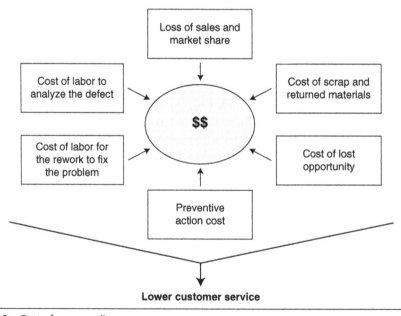

Figure 2.6 Cost of poor quality.

— Review of new product design, development, and test plans
— Providing additional employee training
— Writing new procedures
— Enactment of tools to reduce defects
— Instituting quality improvement programs
— Implementing quality audits
— Extra efforts on supplier quality evaluations
— Putting vigor on the governance and accountability, etc.

There are also costs associated with the application of any of the preceding items. In addition, there are other costs associated with:

* *Loss of sales.* The customers who encountered the problems/defects may not give you repeat business and may decide to go to another vendor. Word of mouth travels faster than any advertisement. The word of failures in a product is usually repeated to friends and family members, thus discouraging them to conduct potential trade with you. There may be customer defection, which has a direct effect on profit.

* *Loss of market share.* It will be difficult to attract new customers if the news of the problem appears in the local media. New customers are also lost because the word of poor quality has a negative image, and no one wants to deal with a company who has gained a reputation in low-quality products.

* *Lower customer satisfaction.* It is difficult for customers to forget difficulties encountered with the product they paid for, especially if they wasted a lot of valuable time due to the product not working effectively.

There are other hidden costs that are not considered, but these need to be looked at as well:

* Cost associated with downtime of computers and equipment

* Extra customer support costs

* Additional communications required between different functional groups

* Additional documentation required to identify the root causes of the problem

* Warranty costs

* Lost discounts

* Extra customer allowances given to rebuild the relationship

* Loss of goodwill

* Downgrading of product

* Delays

A thorough understanding of the cost of poor quality and the costs associated with product support and product issue escalation is good, but it is not sufficient. New technologies have afforded companies the capabilities to learn about product defects before they are encountered and proactively take actions to remove the associated costs with support and fixes. Industry tends to underestimate the costs associated with the escalation of problems when first-level support cannot provide a fix to the customer.

2.14.1 Support Escalation Process

As mentioned before, the costs associated with support escalation are not generally scrutinized or viewed with in-depth analysis. Even though adequate training is provided to the service representatives, there are times when it is not feasible to solve the reported issue. A support escalation process is a procedure put in place when the customer service group is not able to identify the root cause of the problem reported by the customer. This warrants an escalation to another department such as engineering, where subject matter experts can evaluate the problem further, narrow down the cause, and fix it. A carefully developed escalation process ensures that reported issues do not linger and adversely affect the company.

In the case of software, developers are a precious commodity, and most companies would much rather have them continuously work on code of the new products to take these to the market sooner. For this, customer support is trained to ask the customer detailed questions in order to assist in solving the reported problem. Due to the complexity of software, on many occasions, the engineers receive the escalated problem to fix.

The following list provides an example of the escalation steps for a high-level problem for a software issue encountered by a customer. Note that this is a generic outline, and from company to company, the process defers. In some companies it is just five steps, while in others we have seen more than 20 steps:

1. Customer calls in to customer service, and the issue is logged

2. Technical analyst tries to address the issue and is not successful

3. The issue is escalated to development engineering

4. Customer is notified of the escalation

5. Development engineer is assigned to analyze the issue

6. If multiple development engineering groups worked on the feature where the issue occurred, product management is notified

7. The account manager whose customer reported the issue is notified

8. A team of cross-functional engineers analyze and isolate the problem and provide an estimate of the time needed to fix the issue

9. The customer is contacted and notified as to when to expect the fix

10. The development engineering group whose code is identified as problematic writes new code to fix the problem

11. The code is unit tested and regression tested

12. The fix is sent to the customer

13. The issue ticket is closed

14. Because the root cause was identified during the analysis, corrective and preventive actions are documented, and training is given to avoid a similar problem from occurring again

Reported customer issues and an escalation process add huge expenses to COPQ. We see companies trying to upgrade the technical knowledge of their customer service department on a continual basis and making them aware of the costs associated with poor quality. There are some companies that deploy tiger teams to address customer problems, adding another expense to the overall equation of costs associated with poor quality.

2.14.2 Tiger Teams

The concept of forming *tiger teams* is not new. To ensure speedy response time in addressing a customer-reported problem, companies act swiftly to form a tiger team consisting of a few subject matter experts who investigate problems, recommend solutions, or solve the problems. These cross-functional experts are hand picked by senior management because of their knowledge and expertise. Together, they are brought in to focus on a specific glitch with a goal to solve the issue and develop a solution within a prescribed time frame.

A team lead is assigned to manage the project and ensure the problem is analyzed and a recommendation is developed. Depending on the complexity of the problem, 100% of each member's time is devoted to the project; however, the time may vary.

For a tiger team to succeed, a senior leader as a sponsor for the project is needed because additional funds or resources may be required to fulfill the original goal. Along with their expertise, the members of the tiger team are picked based on the following skills:

• Communication

• Leadership

• Negotiation

• Project management

• Attention to details

• Personal credibility

• Meeting management

Total consensus from all the members of the tiger team is expected on the rec-ommendation. After the analysis of the problem and determination of the recommendation, an estimated timeline for implementing the recommendation is evaluated; resources and the necessary expertise are also taken into consider-ation by the members. Finally, the results are discussed with senior management.

Once senior management buy-in is achieved, a formal project plan is devel-oped with a RACI (responsible, accountable, consulted, and informed) model, identifying the activities and individuals who will address the activities outlined in the project plan. Periodic status meetings are held to ensure the plan is on track.

In summary, to avoid additional costs, increase positive customer experi-ence, and build stronger customer loyalty and company brand, telemetry is one of the methods to proactively address problems and manage customer expectations.

3

Telemetry Data

In this chapter, we walk the reader through the evolutionary journey of data science from its humble beginnings to present uses of telemetry data in creating adaptive experiences. In the first section, we offer a comprehensive review of data, including history, basic structures and databases, organizational approaches, data quality, and data security; we close with a review of the concept of big data. Then we review the data science field and discuss what roles in that field look like. We then get practical and discuss how actionable insights are actually created in the context of customer experience. We follow that with a discussion of creating sustainable customer experience feedback loops. We review another use of data insights in designing products that meet customer expectations from the start. We close with a discussion about using real-time telemetry data and machine-learning algorithms to create an adaptive customer experience.

This chapter is organized into the following sections:

1. All about data

2. The data scientist

3. Creating actionable insights from metrics

4. Key performance indicators of customer experience

5. Creating a closed loop for improving customer experience

6. Improving customer experience through intentional design

7. Adaptive customer experience through telemetry data

3.1 ALL ABOUT DATA

In this section, we help the reader build a strong foundation of relevant data concepts. The topics include:

- Quick history of data
- Data structures and databases
- Centralized versus decentralized data storage

55

- Data quality

- Data security

- Data protection

- Data classification

- Interested parties for classified data

- Big data

3.1.1 Quick History of Data

In the context of telemetry, *data* is a term used to represent system information. If you do an internet search for the word "data" today, you will find a definition that resembles the following: "Data is the quantities, characters, or symbols on which operations are performed by a computer, being stored and transmitted in the form of electrical signals and recorded on magnetic, optical, or mechanical recording media."[1] However, the history of data precedes the origins of electricity, computers, digital processing, and storage. As human society grew in size and complexity, there was an increasing need to record, store, and process information.

The so-called Ishango Bone,[2] discovered in 1960 in present-day Uganda, represents the earliest evidence of human data recording. This artifact dates back to 18,000 B.C.E. and was used by prehistoric tribes to keep track of supplies and/or trade. The information was captured in the form of carvings into the bone. It is believed these prehistoric people could even carry out primitive calculations by simply comparing these artifacts.

Data recording by humans continued to evolve from its origins in bone carvings. Recording media such as tablets, scrolls, and paper started to be used to capture and store information. Libraries emerged as early versions of information storage facilities. For example, the Library of Alexandria is believed to have stored as many as 500,000 scrolls containing much of the recorded human knowledge of its time.

The development of magnetic tape in 1928 by Fritz Pfleumer ushered in a significant acceleration in the ability of humans to store information. Magnetic tape allowed recording and play back of large volumes of information. I have childhood memories of a device owned by my uncle that relied on large reels of magnetic tape to record and play back music at family events. Over time, the tapes came in different form factors for different applications and recording times. These variations included large magnetic tape reels for computer storage, 8 tracks, and smaller cassettes, among many other sizes/densities. In 1965, magnetic storage technology was used by the U.S. government to establish the world's first data center. That facility was designed to store 745 million tax returns and 175 million sets of fingerprints.[3] Even today, magnetic storage technology continues to play a significant role with its use in computer hard drives.

In the 1980s, optical data storage media made an entrance into the mass market as a means of encoding recorded music in devices known as compact discs (CDs). These devices promised higher information density and smaller form factors when compared with contemporary music storage technologies like vinyl and tape. Evolutions of optical disk storage technology enabled introduction of other mass-market devices like CD-R (read) and CD-RW (read write) discs, which were designed for use in computers. Today, optical storage technology continues to play a critical role in information storage, particularly with regard to recording/playback of music and videos.

In terms of data analysis tools, the emergence of statistics allowed society to significantly expand existing data analysis capability. In 1663, John Graunt started analyzing mortality data in London in the hope this would lead to early detection of bubonic plague outbreaks. Some 200 years later, Henry Furnese demonstrated how insights from structured analysis of business activity data could provide a competitive advantage. This led to the coining of the term *business intelligence* by Richard Millar Devens in the *Encyclopedia of Commercial and Business Anecdotes*.[4]

The abacus, introduced at around 2400 B.C.E. in Babylon, represents perhaps the earliest example of a device specifically designed for data calculations. In the 17th century, the invention of mechanical calculators by Pascal and Schickard[5] marked a big milestone in the evolution of human data processing capability. Mechanical calculators continued to be enhanced over time culminating with devices like the Dalton adding machine at around 1902 (see Figure 3.1).

Specialized (analog) electrical computation machines emerged in the early 20th century. The first digital machines were developed during World War II.

Figure 3.1 Dalton adding machine.

Source: Courtesy of the Early Office Museum (http://www.officemuseum.com).

Solid-state electronic calculators emerged in the 1960s, and pocket-size versions became available a decade later. The processing capacity and sophistication of these devices has continuously increased with dramatic improvements. These devices were the predecessors of today's personal computers (PCs).

In the 1960s, the introduction of computer inter-networking and the use of internet protocol suites led to a paradigm shift in terms of data storage and computational power. The network became the primary source of information and computational power for humans. Specialized algorithms running on the global interconnected computer network (internet), called *search engines*, allowed relatively easy access to large volumes of previously dispersed information.

Summarizing, it is clear that data and our ability to create and capture such information have come a long way from those early bone carvings. Today, data represents the underlying currency of our digital world. Companies compete for access to data, criminals seek to steal data, and individuals continuously create data (willingly or not) as they go through their daily lives in our digitally connected societies.

3.1.2 Data Structures and Databases

Organizing data in a way that eases consumption by humans and/or machines becomes the next hurdle beyond creating and capturing data. In one of the author's home workshop, he takes pride in having a variety of tools that, with adequate training, allow him to undertake many home improvement projects. Unfortunately for him, he lacks the necessary organizational system or catalog to keep track of them. This leads to wasting a lot of time searching for a tool or buying duplicate versions of a tool. Data is in many ways, like those tools in the workshop: without the proper catalog/organizational system, they are useless!

In the previous section, we talked about how ancient libraries were early renditions of large data storage facilities. The Library of Alexandria was said to have contained half a million scrolls of information. Each scroll, in turn, contained a specific set of information created by a scribe about a specific topic or set of topics. The first known library catalog was called Pinakes. It is said to have been developed by Callimachus (310/305–240 B.C.E.) during his tenure at the Library of Alexandria in the 3rd century B.C.E..[6] The collection of scrolls at the Library of Alexandria is said to have been grouped together by subject matter and the scrolls were stored in bins.[7] Each bin carried a label with painted tablets hung above the stored papyri. The Pinakes catalog was a set of index lists named after the painted tablets. The bins gave bibliographical information for every roll.[8] A typical entry started with a title and also provided the author's name, birthplace, father's name, any teachers trained under, and educational background. It contained a brief biography of the author and a list of the author's publications. The entry had the first line of the work, a summary of its contents, the name of the author, and information about the origin of the roll.[9] Variations on the Pinakes system were used in libraries until 1876, when Melvil Dewey developed the Dewey Decimal Classification, which is still in use today.

Nowadays, an organized set of data (like bins in the Library of Alexandria) is referred to as a *database*. The organizational approach or schema (think of the Pinakes system) used in a database is typically designed to model desired elements and support efficient storage/retrieval/processing of information. In other words, the schema specifies what data elements can be part of the database given possible applications and end-user interests. The database schema is typically designed by a database administrator. For example, a company's employee directory database is designed to include information that potential consumers would like to know for a given employee such as phone number, e-mail address, office location, etc.

Data structures provide a means to manage large amounts of data efficiently for uses in databases or manage information from the internet. Usually, the efficiency of a data structure design determines the efficiency of algorithms that process its contents.

There are numerous types of data structures, generally built upon simpler foundational ones. The six most common foundational data elements are[10]:

1. *Array.* Data elements in a specific order, typically all of the same type. Elements are accessed using an integer index to specify which element is required. Arrays may be a fixed length or resizable.

2. *List.* Linear collection of data elements of any type, called nodes, where each node has a value and points to the next node in the linked list. The principal advantage of a linked list over an array is that values can always be efficiently inserted and removed without relocating the rest of the list. However, some other operations, such as random access to a certain element, are slower with lists than arrays.

3. *Record.* An aggregate data structure—in other words, a value that contains other values, typically in fixed number and sequence and typically indexed by names. The elements of records are usually called fields or members.

4. *Union.* Data structure that specifies which of a number of permitted primitive types may be stored in its instances—for example, float or long integer. Contrast with a record, which could be defined to contain a float and an integer, whereas in a union, there is only one value at a time. Enough space is allocated to contain the widest member data type.

5. *Tagged union.* Data structure that contains an additional field indicating its current type, for enhanced type safety.

6. *Class.* Data structure that contains data fields, like a record, as well as various methods that operate on the contents of the record. In the context of object-oriented programming, records are known simply as data structures to distinguish them from classes.

Data structures are used to organize the storage and retrieval of information in both the computer's main memory and secondary memory. They are classified based on the manner the computer uses to retrieve and store data elements in its memory. Specialized software applications called *database management systems* (DBMSs) have been developed to capture and analyze data as they are exchanged between the database itself and the user and other applications. A DBMS allows the creation, definition, querying, update, and management of databases. There are two primary types of database technologies in use today:

- Relational (also known as Structured Query Language—SQL in short) databases

- Nonrelational (also known as NoSQL) databases

3.1.2.1 Relational (SQL) Databases

Relational databases are structured and allow you to easily find specific information. A key characteristic is that they use tables to store information. Using this type of database, you can generate reports that contain only certain fields from each record and sort based on any field. The basic structure of a table is comprised of rows and columns. In a relational database, standard data fields are represented as rows, and standard attributes are represented as columns. The elements within a given row are, by definition, related. The fields are attribute types of the data and, again, are represented as columns. The relationship between the field types and the tables is known as the schema. Structured Query Language (SQL) is a type of DBMS. It is essentially a programing language used by database administrators to design/manage relational databases. Some of the most popular SQL databases include MySQL, Oracle, IMB DB2, and Sybase.

3.1.2.2 Nonrelational (NoSQL) Databases

The basic unit of organization in a nonrelational database is the document (some NoSQL databases are designed around key values, columns, and graphs instead of documents), so these systems are often referred as document oriented. They also tend to be distributed across computers. A flat file containing delimited data is an example of a nonrelational database. Storing/retrieving data from this type of database is often very fast and does not require table schemas. This type of database is perfect for applications involving very large amounts of unstructured data (from sensors, internet applications, etc.) whose characteristics are not clearly understood and, therefore, require a great deal of flexibility. Examples of popular NoSQL databases include MongoDB, Apache's CouchDB, HBase, and Oracle NoSQL. The particular suitability of a given NoSQL database depends on the problem it is designed to solve. Even though these data stores are seen as more flexible than their SQL counterparts, barriers to greater adoption exist, including:

- Need to use low-level query commands

- Lack of standardized interfaces

- Huge previous investments in existing relational databases

Database administrators use specific criteria when deciding which type of database to use. Figure 3.2 summarizes the characteristics of both relational and nonrelational databases.

In her article called "SQL vs. NoSQL Databases: What's the Difference?" Cary Wodehouse summarizes the main reasons to select one versus the other as follows[11]:

Reasons to use an SQL database

1. *You need to ensure ACID (atomicity, consistency, isolation, and durability) compliancy.* ACID compliancy reduces anomalies and protects the integrity of your database by prescribing exactly how transactions interact with the database. Generally, NoSQL databases sacrifice ACID compliancy for flexibility and processing speed, but for many e-commerce and financial applications, an ACID-compliant database remains the preferred option.

2. *Your data is structured and unchanging.* If your business is not experiencing massive growth that would require more servers and you're only working with data that's consistent, then there may be no reason to use a system designed to support a variety of data types and high traffic volume.

Reasons to use a NoSQL database

1. *Storing large volumes of data that often have little to no structure.* A NoSQL database sets no limits on the types of data you can store together, and allows you to add different new types as your needs change. With document-based databases, you can store data in one place without having to define what "types" of data those are in advance.

2. *Making the most of cloud computing and storage.* Cloud-based storage is an excellent cost-saving solution, but requires data to be easily spread across

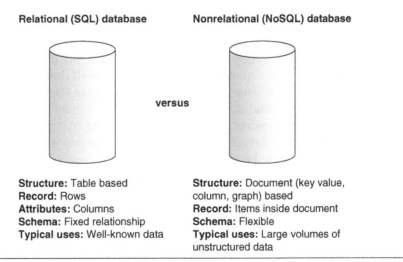

Relational (SQL) database   **Nonrelational (NoSQL) database**

versus

Structure: Table based | **Structure:** Document (key value, column, graph) based
Record: Rows | **Record:** Items inside document
Attributes: Columns | **Schema:** Flexible
Schema: Fixed relationship | **Typical uses:** Large volumes of
Typical uses: Well-known data | unstructured data

Figure 3.2   Relational versus nonrelational databases.

multiple servers to scale up. Using commodity (affordable, smaller) hardware on-site or in the cloud saves you the hassle of additional software, and NoSQL databases like Cassandra are designed to be scaled across multiple data centers out of the box without a lot of headaches.

3. *Rapid development.* If you're developing within two-week agile sprints, cranking out quick iterations, or needing to make frequent updates to the data structure without a lot of downtime between versions, a relational database will slow you down. NoSQL data doesn't need to be prepped ahead of time.

Summarizing, data needs to be organized in a way that makes storage and consumption by humans or machines efficient. The foundational building blocks used to organize data are known as data structures. Organized sets of data are known as databases. Database management systems (DBMSs) help orchestrate the exchanges among users, databases, and applications. Databases are classified into relational or nonrelational, depending on how data is stored and organized in computer memory.

3.1.3 Centralized versus Decentralized Data Storage

A centralized database is one in which the data is stored and maintained in a single location. This location will correspond to where the processing (CPU) and storage (memory) components of the computer system are located. For example, in a personal computer, a local database would exist in the computer's CPU and memory. Users can access the local database through a local interface or through remote applications running through the interconnected computer network.

In the early days of computing (circa late 1950s), computer systems did not have interactive interfaces capable of supporting multiple users. Instead, these early systems operated in single threaded mode, and they only accepted input data in the form of punched cards or magnetic tape. By the early 1970s, computer systems had evolved to support interactive interfaces, operate in timesharing mode, and support many users simultaneously. Users gained access to the systems through devices called computer terminals. So, the initial databases and corresponding database management systems were all designed to operate in a centralized computer system. Even after the advent of the personal computer, devices ran terminal emulation software that allowed them to remotely connect and consume the processing and storage power of the central computer system.

However, as PCs became increasingly more popular and capable, local processing and storage became more widespread, particularly with consumers and small enterprises. New types of database management systems were developed with the local computer in mind. Still, centralized computing and storage remained in use, particularly with larger enterprises and/or government agencies.

A distributed data storage system relies on information stored on more than one computer, often with a certain replication capability. Some distributed databases expose rich query abilities, while others are limited to key-value store semantics. Distributed databases are usually nonrelational databases that make a quick access to data over a large number of computers. These computers could be collocated in a data center or distributed across geographies.

Network virtualization (see Figure 3.3), together with the pervasiveness of reliable, worldwide computer inter-networking, propelled the emergence of cloud computing, which shares certain similarities with the central computing systems of old because it acts as a single processing and storage unit. However, cloud computing is realized across the global internet, providing shared processing, memory, and data to remote computers and other devices on demand. It provides access to a pool of configurable computing resources like networking, storage, servers, services, and applications. Cloud computing powered by network virtualization is the most pervasive network architecture on the internet today.

Designers of large distributed data stores typically chose to compromise consistency in favor of availability, partition tolerance, and speed. The reason for that is that high-speed read/write access results in reduced consistency because it is not possible to have consistency, availability, and partition tolerance of the system, as it has been proven by the consistency availability partition (CAP) theorem (see Figure 3.4).

Network virtualization is a technology that allows the combination of distinct networking, processing, and storage resources into one software-based entity known as a virtual network. Virtualization allows these systems to act as a centralized entity even if underlying components reside in different computers that are either colocated or not.

Figure 3.3 Network virtualization.

CAP is a very influential principle in the design of distributed databases. Also known as Brewer's theorem (after computer scientist Eric Brewer), it states that it is impossible for a distributed data store to simultaneously provide more than two out of the following three guarantees[1]:

- **Consistency:** Every read receives the most recent write (or an error message)
- **Availability:** Every request receives a response, although it does not guarantee that it contains the most recent write
- **Partition:** The system continues to operate despite an arbitrary number of messages being dropped (or delayed) by the network

Given that no distributed system is completely immune from network failures, network partitioning generally has to be tolerated. In the presence of a partition, one is then left with two options: consistency or availability. When choosing consistency over availability, the system will return an error or a time-out if particular information cannot be guaranteed to be up-to-date due to network partitioning. When choosing availability over consistency, the system will always process the query and try to return the most recent available version of the information, even if it cannot guarantee it is up-to-date due to network partitioning.[2] It is important to remember that the CAP theorem does not preclude that both availability and consistency can be concurrently satisfied in the absence of network failure (i.e., during normal operating conditions).

Figure 3.4 Consistency availability partition (CAP) theorem.

[1]Seth Gilbert and Nancy Lynch, "Brewer's conjecture and the feasibility of consistent, available, partition-tolerant web services," *ACM SIGACT News*, 33 no. 2 (2002), pp. 51–59; "Brewer's CAP theorem," http://julianbrowne .com, retrieved March 2, 2010; "Brewers CAP theorem on distributed systems," http://royans.net.

[2]Armando Fox and Eric Brewer, "Harvest, yield and scalable tolerant systems," *Proc. 7th Workshop Hot Topics in Operating Systems (HotOS 99)*, IEEE CS, 1999, pp. 174–178.

These large distributed data stores are mostly implemented using NoSQL databases, and they offer the concept of "eventual consistency." This means that database changes are propagated to all nodes "eventually" (typically in the order of milliseconds). Requests for data might not return the latest (updated) record immediately or might result in reading data that is not accurate. This data inaccuracy issue is known as *stale reads*.[12] Additionally, NoSQL systems may exhibit lost writes and other forms of data loss.[13] Fortunately, some NoSQL systems provide concepts such as write-ahead logging to avoid data loss.[14] For distributed transaction processing across multiple databases, data consistency is an even bigger challenge that is difficult for both NoSQL and relational databases.

Figure 3.5 visually describes the differences between centralized and decentralized systems. In the case of centralized systems, all users are served from a centralized single resource (central node). In the case of decentralized systems, users are served by several resources that, in turn, are interconnected. Distributed users are served by multiple resources that are highly interconnected.

Summarizing, cloud and network virtualization technologies have really blurred the lines between consuming resources from a centralized versus a decentralized computing/storage system. However, physical dispersions of the type seen in today's cloud-based data stores are particularly vulnerable (when compared to centralized counterparts) to network failures. Because decentralized systems rely on the network to interconnect components of their virtualized computer system, any network failure can cause that system to become inconsistent. In the case of a centralized system, the network is the means for users to access the resources of the computer system. So, network failures will translate to user availability issues not database corruption issues.

3.1.4 Data Quality

Data is considered a perishable commodity. This means that data become obsolete if not regularly refreshed/updated. The frequency of the updates will depend on the nature of the information. Here is a personal example. One of the authors enjoys running to keep feeling healthy, and uses a wearable device to help track distance, pace, cadence, etc. If the wearable device were to communicate his data

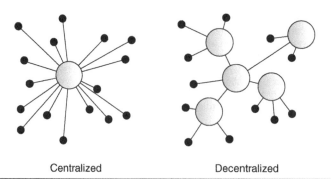

Centralized   Decentralized

Figure 3.5 Centralized versus decentralized.

with a one-day (or even one-hour) delay, it would make the data completely useless because he could not use the information to adjust my pace in real time, which is a big part of why the device was purchased in the first place.

The term *data quality* refers to the condition of a set of values of qualitative or quantitative variables. Data is considered high quality if it is fit for its intended uses in decision making, operations, and planning. As data volumes increase, the question of internal (to database) data consistency becomes an important element of data quality as well. *Data cleansing* is the term used to describe actions applied to a given data set to improve its quality.

International Organization for Standardization (ISO) standard ISO 9000:2015 defines *quality* as the extent to which a set of characteristics fulfills requirements. By extension, we could define *data quality* as the extent to which a *set of data characteristics* fulfills the *database user requirements*. Requirements are defined as the need or expectation that is stated, generally implied, or obligatory.

Data characteristics include:

- Completeness

- Validity

- Accuracy

- Consistency

- Availability

- Timeliness

The interest in data quality started from the early days of the computer era. The U.S. government decided to build and maintain a database containing people's name and address information. The objective was to help the U.S. Postal Service ensure mail was delivered to the correct destination. Rules were built into the database to track common data inconsistencies such as misspellings or typos in name and address information and those caused by life-changing events (married, moved, new job, etc.).

The U.S. government started sharing this "validated" information with private companies to help cross-reference their data through the National Change of Address registry. It became quickly apparent to participating companies that these validation efforts helped them save millions of dollars in otherwise manual correction efforts. This realization provided the necessary impetus for corporations to start their own data quality efforts.

Data quality is now recognized as a critical businesses function. Leading companies dedicate whole departments within their information technology (IT) functions to improving data quality. A key focus for these teams is a process called *data quality assurance* (QA in short). This process seeks to assess the following characteristics of data:

- Accuracy

- Consistency

- Confidence bands

- Precisions

- Completeness

Test cases are created to evaluate different aspects of the data against expectations. Test cases are typically executed manually the first time but then automated to ensure sustainable coverage. Data found not to conform to expectations is quarantined (if it can be repaired) or deprecated if not fixable. Branding is applied to data that have gone through a QA process and the data is deemed consumable relative to validation criteria. This branding process becomes a key differentiator between providers of business intelligence data because consumers will tend to avoid data whose source, governance, and integrity cannot be ascertained.

There is a subset of data existing within an enterprise that is critical to the way the organization operates; such data is typically referred to as *reference data*. Reference data, in turn, is administered by IT using the master data management (MDM) system. During QA, data attributes involving reference data are validated against a well-defined set of values to discover discrepancies.

Also, as data is transformed within the enterprise, timestamps are created and captured to create a chain of evidence. These timestamps enable checks to assess data shelf life and improve policies on data movement. Data QA staff require a high degree of business knowledge and acumen. As issues are discovered, they are expected to help formulate changes in data management policy and strategy.

In addition to the quality assurance efforts just discussed, another significant priority is *data governance*. This process seeks to ensure that important data assets are formally managed throughout the enterprise. The key elements of a data governance process include identification of:

1. *Sources of truth.* Where a particular data set originates before it gets transformed

2. *Data steward.* Individual responsible for reviewing and authorizing use of a particular data set within the enterprise

3. *Data normalization process.* Steps needed to convert raw data into information consumable in data marts within the enterprise

4. *Counting rules.* The set of filters and mathematical functions applied to a data set in order to create a metric

5. *Reference data.* Data that identify and manage data elements critical to the operating rhythm of the enterprise

All these elements are by-products of a properly empowered governing body. Later in this chapter, we discuss how to go about establishing a governing body in your enterprise.

Summarizing, enterprises invest considerable resources in ensuring that the information they are using is fit for consumption. Processes such as data quality assurance and governance are examples of the specific activities designed to ensure data quality. There are also cases where the quality of the data is deliberately compromised with criminal intent. These cases are in the realm of data security, which we cover in the next section.

3.1.5 Data Security

In recent times, information security (or cybersecurity) has become a huge concern. Cybercriminals (or hackers), competitors, or unfriendly government-sponsored actors are continuously evolving their ability to infiltrate, disrupt, steal, hijack, and destroy enterprise data warehouses. The phenomenon called *ransomware* is becoming increasingly pervasive across personal, government, and private enterprises. Ransomware involves criminals obtaining information, encrypting it, and then denying access to owners until they are paid a monetary ransom. The U.S. Federal Bureau of Investigation's (FBI) Crime Complaint Center estimated that a single ransomware software attack known as "CryptoWall," which occurred between April 2014 and June 2015, cost Americans more than $18 million. The money was spent not only on ransoms, which ranged from $200 to $10,000 apiece, but also on "network mitigation, network countermeasures, loss of productivity, legal fees, IT services, and/or the purchase of credit monitoring services for employees or customers."

Enterprises are responding to data threats with ever-increasing focus and investment on information security. These efforts go beyond simply reacting to attacks and can be grouped into the following areas:

* *Design.* The data infrastructure (network, servers, and databases) is designed to be resilient to cyberattack. Networks are designed with multilayer defense in mind. This ensures that even if one portion of the network is compromised, access to the rest of the network is not guaranteed. Network address translation (NAT) has been used for many years as a way to protect local area networks from the internet. Additionally, policies and procedures governing passwords are strictly enforced. For example, access to wireless network infrastructure requires password authentication. Finally, use of data encryption is widespread as a final line of defense to prevent unauthorized use of information.

* *Monitoring.* Operation centers are staffed around the clock to oversee traffic and data consumption patterns. Detection capabilities are continuously being enhanced to keep pace with the ever-improving intrusion capabilities of cybercriminals. Once detection is verified, information is shared with a response team to activate countermeasures.

* *Response.* Working closely with the monitoring resources, this area focuses on defining and implementing a playbook of responses to cyberattacks. A typical response involves isolating the portion of the network that has been compromised. Sometimes, active responses can be undertaken where the specific source of the attack is identified. These responses could include disrupting traffic flow from the offending source or informing law enforcement authorities.

- *Remediation.* Once an attack has been isolated or neutralized, efforts are made to restore the information to its pre-attack state; if not possible, the information is deprecated. Then an investigation is carried out to identify lessons learned and recommend actions that would prevent and/or minimize similar attacks in the future. These lessons learned are typically translated into enhancement policies and procedures.

Propaganda and misinformation—particularly around news—are becoming quite pervasive on the internet today. The source of the bogus information is usually not clear, but it is designed to look and feel real. The intent seems to be to discredit legitimate information sources, create confusion, mislead, and create apathy. This trend is one that will require considerable attention going forward, and it is expected to foster development of source validation techniques not available today.

Summarizing, data security is one of the top concerns of network/data administrators today. A significant number of resources are dedicated to ensuring information security. Propaganda and misinformation on the internet are emerging trends that require increased focus going forward.

3.1.6 Data Protection

Collecting data automatically requires that the data be protected and secured. Any individual or company dealing with data needs to understand and conform to a set of rules and standards. These standards define how the data is to be protected and handled as the data move from one place to another or between one person and another.

Here are a few golden rules relative to data protection:

- Data protection standards must be adhered to because they outline the need and necessity of how your company should protect data throughout its life cycle. It should cover all aspects of the data life cycle starting from collection all the way to the destruction of the data.

- All employees, contractors, and temporary workers, as well as anyone else associated with data, must go through mandatory data protection training.

- Data protection starts with classification of data and how various roles are associated with classified data. All employees must be made aware of the need for confidentiality, preservation of data integrity, and rules governing the sharing of data.

3.1.7 Data Classification

Protecting data is everyone's job, and no industry practitioner can consider himself/herself excluded from this responsibility. More than a technology issue, data protection is a process and policy compliance activity. It involves protecting the systems and individual data transactions by dealing with the humans who manage/access the data. In order to identify, classify, and attach the appropriate level of importance to the data being handled, industry standard definitions have been evolving over time. Here are some of those classifications based on various parameters including legal and financial implications:

- *Public data.* This refers to the data that can be transmitted outside of the organizational boundaries without prior permission and can be made available to a publicly viewable domain

- *Confidential.* This set of data is only available internally to company users and not allowed for public consumption; it cannot be shared without leadership approval

- *Highly confidential.* This data is only available to a limited set of users within the company and is controlled by access restrictions

- *Restricted.* This type of data is not available for sharing, and its access is restricted only to those individuals with a *need to know* as identified by the policy makers of the company

Depending on the confidentiality and classification level associated with the data, different encryption methods can be used for storage. For example, restricted data must always be stored with the highest level of encryption and can never be accessed without proper authorization.

Additional regulations affecting collection, storage, and usage of data are regularly being introduced in every country and jurisdiction. One such piece of legislation is the General Data Protection Regulation (GDPR), a data protection program defined by the European Union (EU). GDPR will replace the many existing policies enacted at the national level by EU member states. It is expected to improve the consistency and effectiveness of data protection going forward by limiting the ability of member states to introduce rules at the national level. This consistency will simplify relations with all data protection authorities (DPAs). Member states will participate in the EU-wide process through a single DPA to which they will be primarily accountable. What this legislation (and others similar to it) means to a telemetry ecosystem is more and more considerations to account for while dealing with data.

3.1.8 Interested Parties for Classified Data

There are a number of individuals who deal with classified data. The success of any telemetry project involving classified data requires a proper definition of these roles and their responsibilities and making sure each of these individuals is aware of his or her responsibilities. These roles are:

- *Stakeholders.* Any individuals or organizations involved in the overall data-sharing domain.

- *Data steward.* Usually referred to as the primary owner of the data. They hold the highest level of responsibility and accountability for deciding who can read and write the data.

- *Data producers.* This is where the data gets generated. This is also known as the source of truth.

- *Data consumers.* The individuals who ultimately use the data to drive continuous improvement action, make financial decisions, interpret data trends, or figure out the actions that must be taken.

3.1.9 Big Data

There is an information collection explosion happening across our modern world. Electronic machines and information-sensing devices of different types are being designed to "share" some or all of the information they collect to remote servers through the internet. These include mobile devices, aerial imagery, software logs, cameras, microphones, radio-frequency identification (RFID) readers, and wireless sensor networks. The collection of a large volume of data from traditional or digital sources—structured or unstructured, outside your organization or inside—is known as *big data*, and the place where such data is stored is known as a *data lake*. The information that cannot be easily interpreted by databases or data models is unstructured data. Your digital financial records, driving records, health records, etc., are part of the big data. In the era of the Internet of Things (IoT) we live in, the data may be collected from automobiles, airplanes, grocery stores, interactions over mobile devices, and hundreds of other avenues. All of these data elements together are also known as big data.

The benefit of big data is not derived simply from collection. But the techniques of analyzing the data, interpreting it, and then putting it to use for better causes allow for tremendous advantages. Once you start looking at the data, you will learn about things you are not aware of, and you will be inspired to solve the problems that you see through the data. Data scientists and others are beginning to realize the potential of channeling the data into actionable information that can be used to identify the needs of customers, doctors, market researchers, and others.

Big data presents data processing challenges that traditional applications are incapable of handling. The challenges include transport, analysis, storage, visualization, privacy, data sovereignty, mining, etc. But in addition to challenges, there are plenty of opportunities as well, particularly when using this data to derive actionable insights. For instance, vending machines that regularly report their inventory can be stocked at intervals that match consumption patterns. You could even use this information to decide what the most consumed products are and shift the stock profile to match that.

Big data volumes are typically beyond the capabilities of SQL-based (or relational) database management systems and desktop-based analytical and visualization packages. Storing and processing this information is the purview of distributed storage and processing systems involving hundreds (if not thousands) of computer systems. Big data doctrine encompasses unstructured, semistructured, and structured data. However, the main focus is still on unstructured data.[15] The data dimensions that would be considered the domain of big data are a constantly evolving target, ranging from a few dozen terabytes to many petabytes of data (as of 2018).[16]

In his 2001 paper titled "3D Data Management: Controlling Data Volume, Velocity and Variety," Douglas Laney defined data growth challenges and opportunities associated with big data as having three primary dimensions[17]:

- *Volume* refers to the quantity of generated and stored data. The size of the data determines the value and potential insight and whether it can actually be considered big data or not.

- *Velocity* refers to the speed at which data can be inputted or retrieved. It incorporates the characteristics of timeliness or latency. For instance, is the data being captured at a rate or with a lag time that makes it useful? Also associated with velocity is the shelf life of data. Is it permanently valuable or does it rapidly age and lose its meaning and importance? Understanding this aspect of velocity allows the database administrator to decide what data is no longer meaningful and needs to be discarded.

- *Variety* refers to the range of data types and sources that needs to be supported.

Today, Gartner and much of the information technology industry continue to use this "3Vs" model for describing big data.

To illustrate how big data can be used to improve productivity and efficiency, let's use the following example for the shipping industry:

> If you are working for a shipping company, you can collect data from local facilities on road conditions from the department of transportation to make you aware of any accidents on the routes used for shipping and data from the national weather service to see if there is rain in the forecast. After analyzing all the these data sets, you will schedule your deliveries choosing the roads that have no traffic or accidents and choose the right type of vehicle that can withstand heavy rain if that is in the chosen delivery route. Just this simple analysis can save the delivery drivers time to deliver and speed up the productivity and efficiency of the end-to-end system.

3.1.9.1 Big Data Platform

Leading companies typically have an IT platform that serves as the single solution for features and capabilities needed in developing, operating, and managing a big data environment/infrastructure. The platform usually consists of databases, servers, and storage. However, in some cases, it can also connect to dashboards. The key advantage of having such an IT platform is eliminating the complexity of having various vendors and multiple solutions.

3.2 DATA SCIENTISTS

Now that we have built a good understanding of all aspects of data (definition, structures, databases, architecture, quality, security, and big data), we are ready to talk about the people whose job it is to process all of this data. These individuals are practitioners in an interdisciplinary field known as *data science* and are known as *data scientists*. They are asked to master the scientific methods, processes, and systems needed to extract knowledge or insights from data in various forms, either structured or unstructured.[18] Data science builds on theory and practice from many fields including mathematics, statistics, information science, and computer science.

The typical responsibilities of a data scientist include:

- Finding and understanding rich data sources

- Developing visualizations to help data consumption

- Building mathematical models using the data

- Blending data sources

- Ensuring database consistency

- Managing large amounts of data in highly constrained environments

- Presenting and communicating the data insights/findings

Given the relative short life expectancy of data in the digital world, data scientists are often expected to generate results in days rather than weeks or months. Like their cousins in software engineering, data scientists tend to operate in iterative fashion. This means that they tend to start by conducting an exploration of data; after drawing an initial conclusion based on that assessment, they decide how to proceed. Their work product tends to be dashboards (to display data) and algorithms.

Because of the increasingly important role data plays in our digital world, it is not surprising that data science has turned into an attractive and well-sought-after activity. In fact, *Harvard Business Review* has designated this profession the "Sexiest Job of the 21st Century,"[19] and McKinsey & Company is projecting a global demand of 1.5 million new data scientists.[20] Academia and the private sector have also jumped into this opportunity. Universities are offering master's-level classes in data science.[21] Private companies are offering data science certificates based on successful completion of a data science boot camp.[22]

For those in the data science field, there are handsome rewards given the high demand of the role. These include:

1. *Attractive starting salaries.* In 2017, Glassdoor estimated the average *starting* salary of a data scientist in the United States to be $113,436!

2. *Exciting problem spaces.* Given the broad adoption of big data across the world, you are bound to find an opportunity to use your expertise in an

area of personal interest. This could range from space exploration to navigation to health to food science to education, and so forth.

3. *Visible roles.* Given the nature of the work, data scientists are often asked to present their findings and insights to key decision makers in their enterprise. That type of exposure is likely to translate into opportunities for career advancement.

Data science has several sub-specialties like machine learning, classification, cluster analysis, data mining, databases, and visualization. As you consider roles in the industry, you tend to see job descriptions that emphasize some sub-specialties more than others. Additionally, you will need a strong foundation in the following areas:

- *Database management tools expertise.* This includes SQL programing skills and statistical analysis tools like R.

- *Statistics.* Understanding of basic concepts like mean, median, and standard deviation; different type of statistical distributions; and statistical tests.

- *Calculus and linear algebra.* A basic understanding of these mathematical principles is necessary to successfully perform data analysis using off-the-shelf tools and to optimize algorithms.

- *Communications.* This is particularly important to those responsible for sharing insights with the rest of the company. An inability to communicate effectively is a hindrance to the use and impact of data insights.

Looking at the job descriptions, data science roles tend to fall into one of the following categories:

- The *data analyst* position requires expertise in databases, data classification, visualization, and data mining. The role here tends to be about extracting and organizing data sets.

- The *data engineer* position requires expertise in networking, databases, and data clusters. The focus on this role tends to be constructing the enterprise's data infrastructure.

- The *data scientist* position requires expertise in hard sciences like math, physics, and statistical analysis. This role tends to be focused on the development of algorithms and/or data services.

- The *data generalist* position requires broad expertise across all data science disciplines. The role tends to be focused on the application of data science skills to specific business roles like finance, accounting, HR, sales, etc.

Finally, there is an emerging trend to create a C-suite role focused on data science called *chief data scientist* (CDS). These executives work closely with the chief information officer (CIO) of the company, but their primary responsibility is to look after the data assets of the company. More than looking at the data infrastructure, a CDS ensures the company is poised to handle any influx of data, is able to analyze it, and has a clear path to turn the data into actionable insights. A CDS also has a responsibility for developing machine-learning algorithms and associated innovations that enable the company to process data real time. In fact, reducing time-to-insight is a key driver of the CDS. Companies can no longer afford to follow the traditional approach of presenting insights at quarterly business reviews and relying on follow-up action items. The CDS's development of data-processing algorithms will allow the company to respond quickly to changes.

Leading companies are focused on digitizing the operating processes. Having the ability to process data real time is not a nice-to-have capability but a requirement. The pace of innovation required is staggering, so let's illustrate with this specific example. In the field of customer success, customer experience management is projecting an increase in the ability to create and activate algorithms to process customer data from half a dozen a year to half a dozen a day!

3.2.1 Telemetry and Data Science

Data science and telemetry are often paired as two sides of a coin. We now examine some aspects of these two terms and make a few observations from our experience.

The output of a telemetry infrastructure without data science would be a large mountain of data. However, with data science involved, the output of a telemetry infrastructure will be insights derived from the data collected. This is a good way to think about these two activities. Data science is the larger activity, and telemetry is a use case of data science. Any domain that receives and uses data is considered a client of data science.

3.2.2 Data Scientist and Data Science—Telemetry Use Cases

More and more information technology professionals are focusing on the usage of data and how it can be applied to decision making. It is a common myth that anyone who deals with data is a data scientist. However, if an individual is the one who works in partnership with a business user to translate data into practical and meaningful insights for decision makers, that person is a data scientist. While there is a side of data science that involves mathematical modeling, formulas, and statistical equations, we do not consider such expertise as sufficient to classify someone as a data scientist. The following list defines a few use cases that should help further clarify the reader's understanding of data science:

- *Use case 1.* In an edge device, the CPU is hitting 80% utilization every day at a given interval and generating an alert. What inference can be made from this information? Can the situation be managed proactively and perhaps avoid the creation of an alarm if the data can be converted into an automatic corrective action?

- *Use case 2*. Using data collected and processed from more than 10,000 end nodes over the past three months, can we find out feature usage by geography and determine how to present the information to end users to enable action? Is there any specific usage pattern that can be gleaned for these users, and is there a possibility of targeted marketing that focuses on these users based on analysis? Is there a possibility of predictive analytics and market penetration strategy from the data and insights, and how can such insights be useful for the sales and marketing team?

- *Use case 3*. In a given geography, what would be the next one-year potential adoption of a specific software feature of a product based on the previous nine-months' usage patterns? What forecast can the engineering department use to adjust its workforce and training strategy based on such analytics?

- *Use case 4*. Given the current rate of quality issues reported, what would be a feasible period for the product to reach maturity in terms of defect rate? Can there be an automatic injection of such insights into the engineering workflow to alert the department to potential resource and budget commitments needed to satisfy the quality objectives?

- *Use case 5*. Given the current feature's usage and customer adoption, when should the next upgrade cycle be scheduled, and what product mix would bring the best usage of the product? Can we predict a potential network outage or network congestion based on peak hour traffic and proactively notify the relevant planning department?

- *Use case 6*. How many software licenses are purchased, and how are they being utilized? From the usage pattern, can we identify which licenses should be avoided in the next purchase cycle, thereby creating a trusting relationship between the seller and the buyer? How can a software-based revenue stream and a recurring revenue target be predicted from such insights?

- *Use case 7*. In a given code base, is it possible to identify a potential collateral regression defect based on the line of code modified? Can such analysis be extended to workflow automation and used to stop a vulnerable code from customer release, thereby reducing the risk of customer-found defects?

- *Use case 8*. Based on the customer issues received, can we determine which ones will likely have the biggest impact on overall customer satisfaction? Which defect has the highest potential to get escalated? What additional defects can be collateral to the current one and thereby be avoided in the future?

Similar to these, there are many more use cases that can be developed. The imagination is really the limit on what use cases can be defined. Without well-thought-out uses cases, the data scientist's work will not be very helpful. What makes the data and data scientist smart and accountable are the practical wisdom and usage of the data, and how these insights are then translated into actions in the organization. Without the partnership among a business user, data, and data scientist, the entire telemetry infrastructure would be useless.

3.3 CREATING ACTIONABLE INSIGHTS FROM METRICS

Now that we have a good foundation of data and the data science field, it is time for us to discuss how we actually go about turning data into actionable insights. If you reflect on it, it may seem like a straightforward proposition: we have the data, so what else do we need? Collecting, storing, and visualizing the data seem hard enough! Unfortunately, we need more: we need business knowledge.

Business knowledge comes as a result of having experience and a deep understanding of the business and operating model of the enterprise. For example, if you work at a hardware store, business knowledge involves understanding the needs of your market, your competition, your differentiated value, and the set of processes used to run your enterprise. Once you have business knowledge, you could then make observations (through data, say) and turn them into valuable insights. For instance, you would start by observing that there is a certain product in the store whose inventory tends to runs out two days after restocking. By understanding your market, you are confident that there is a demand for this product that is not being met. You share the results of your analysis and make a recommendation to change the stocking profile for the product and, therefore, satisfy that unmet demand.

Fortunately, there is a way to encapsulate business knowledge into standard models that can be used by individuals or machines with limited or no understanding of the business to create insights; those models are called *metrics*. Metrics are created by applying certain rules (counting rules) to underlying data to make their trend behavior more predictable. For example, you can take customer call data (volume, product, and resolution code) and create a metric that helps you understand if customer experience with a software element of a product is getting (i.e., trending) better, worse, or the same. Once you have such a metric defined (which requires business knowledge), monitoring the trend does not require the same level of business knowledge. In fact, you could fully automate the analysis by creating an algorithm that processes the underlying data, applies statistical process control, and raises an alarm when the metric starts moving outside of a predefined control zone.

"What gets measured gets done" is the phrase that tells the story. Metrics are defined to support the business and specific areas that need attention. So, deciding where metrics are needed always starts with business requirements that specify what aspects of the business require monitoring. Like other critical aspects of the business, agreed-upon metrics will help in evaluating overall performance of the business and quality management system effectiveness; at the same time, it will answer two critical questions:

1. What aspect of the business needs improvement?

2. Is the improvement activity having the desired effect once action has been taken?

Metrics affect all the phases of the life cycle and typically are carried out by different functional areas. Achieving cross-functional agreement on metrics can be challenging because each function would like to define and control its own area. A good practice here is to have a neutral third party (an outside entity or corporate function) responsible for defining and driving the key performance indicators; this is similar to the role that corporate finance plays for other business indicators. However, the definition and management of the metrics needs to be done in a transparent and collaborative fashion.

A dashboard that shows trends for each of these metrics can be used to drive governance discussions during functional and management reviews. It is important to integrate quality and customer experience insights into the rhythm of how the business runs. A balanced scorecard approach is frequently used to run the business. These scorecards are used as a part of regular operations reviews and the scorecard tends to be organized into four quadrants:

1. *Financial.* This quadrant of the scorecard reflects information showing the financial health of the organization. Typical metrics include revenue trends, market share, profitability, outstanding debts, and so forth.

2. *Operations.* This quadrant reflects information showing how efficiently the organization runs. This includes the policies and processes established from beginning to end for design and development such as controls, outsourcing, traceability, and nonconformance. Among others, the metrics include production levels relative to capacity, speed of innovation, and so forth.

3. *People.* This quadrant reflects information showing the trends and status for people-relevant indicators. Typical metrics here include attrition rate, hiring trends, span of control, employee engagement, and so forth.

4. *Customer.* This quadrant reflects information showing the health of the customer relationships. This is where customer experience and quality data will be shown.

Different types of metrics are needed in order to manage different aspects of the business. It is imperative to use the right metric for the right purpose, or it can lead to inaction and/or endless debate. For example, trying to use the "check engine" message on your car dashboard to diagnose a problem with the engine can be frustrating. This metric can tell you that there is something wrong with the engine, but it can't help you analyze the problem any further. You need additional data to do that.

Unfortunately, there is no perfect metric when it comes to balancing breadth and depth of information. For example, strategic metrics tend to provide a broader or general view of customer experience, but because of their broad nature, they lack sufficient specificity to drive action. Likewise, you can have metrics that can give you actionability but lack the broad perspective of a strategic metric. Trying to build actionability into strategic metrics can be a frustrating exercise. Our recommendation is to realize that you need different metrics for different objectives and, therefore, to understand what you have and what you need.

3.4 KEY PERFORMANCE INDICATORS OF CUSTOMER EXPERIENCE

Similar to our earlier discussion about reference data in the context of master data management, you need a minimum set of metrics that, as a whole, give you a good understanding of how the business (or process) you are monitoring is performing. This set of metrics is known as *key performance indicators*. In the context of customer experience management, they can be organized into three main groups.

3.4.1 Customer Sentiment Metrics

This first group measures customer sentiment, loyalty, or perception. It measures the customer's emotional state, asking "how the customer feels" upon experiencing any interaction with the organization, ranging from watching an advertisement to using a product or service. This information is essential to engage in a business transaction with the organization. As a consumer, you likely will avoid merchants that engender negative feelings, particularly if you have alternative vendors.

Historically, customer satisfaction (CSAT) has been used as the primary indicator of customer perception. CSAT is measured on a scale from 1 to 5, where 5 is best and 1 is worst. The feedback is provided by customers through surveys that include questions that refer to key aspects of the customer experience. For example, customers might be asked to rate their level of satisfaction with technical support from 1 to 5. Survey administration is done in such a way that you can capture a statistically significant sample of your total customer base. You also need to track the respondents to the survey based on their role within the customer context—buyer or user, executive or administrator, and so forth. Finally, you need to appropriately segment the responses based on market, geography, and so forth.

In addition to the numerical score, CSAT surveys typically include a free-form component (verbatim) where customers have the option to provide additional comments to support their score. In our experience, verbatim analysis or text analytics can be frequently overlooked in light of the quantifiable nature of numerical scores. However, this information is important in lending a customer voice to metrics such that change agents can be used to drive action and create empathy.

Over the past few years, an increasing number of organizations have moved from CSAT-based measures of loyalty toward Net Promoter Score (NPS™, a registered trademark of Fred Reichheld, Bain & Company, and Satmetrix). NPS asks the customer's "likelihood to recommend" given his or her interactions with the organization. NPS is seen as providing a more direct connection to the business because "recommending" implies a deeper level of advocacy than simply "being satisfied." More importantly, "recommending" is seen as achieving a higher threshold of value level than simply being "satisfied." The logic goes that you could feel satisfied with a product but not enough to recommend whereas you would likely not recommend a product for which you are not satisfied.

Like CSAT, NPS is collected via surveys but customers are provided with a scale of 0 through 10. The lower scores (0–6) are considered detractors. Those in the middle (7–8) are known as passive. Those with higher scores (9–10) are known as promoters. Net Promoter Score is calculated by subtracting the percentage of detractors from the percentage of promoters. The passive contributes toward calculation of total scores (denominator to calculate percentages), but does not otherwise factor in the Net Promoter formula. Like CSAT, NPS also has a free-form section for additional context.

NPS becomes an even stronger indicator when it is correlated with key business indicators such as wallet share, customer acquisition/loss rates, and so forth. Leading companies have discovered that when it comes to doing correlation analysis looking at the NPS score by itself is not very insightful. The preferred approach is to decompose the data into promoters, passives, and detractors, then analyze those trends separately. Rather than averaging across geographies and segments, establishing those correlations at the regional or solution level is proven to be more insightful. A free-form section provides a perfect complement to statistical analysis by providing critical proof points and specific pain points that can be acted upon.

3.4.2 Customer Experience Metrics

The second group measures customer pain/dissatisfaction or friction associated with customer interactions. In the traditional product quality context, friction metrics would be software or hardware failure rates or mean time between failures. Product quality continues to be the foundation of customer experience. However, when considering the totality of customer interactions, friction points could include measures of how difficult it is to get pre-sale information, purchasing process, licensing process, technical support, and so forth. These types of metrics are a good "double-click" on customer sentiment metrics because they get closer to where the customer dissatisfaction is and, therefore, closer to what can be done to mitigate it. Groups inside the organization would use customer experience metrics to track the success of their internal quality improvement initiatives. These metrics are typically used to drive internal accountability to customer experience.

When statistical process control techniques are applied to customer experience metrics, organizations are able to proactively identify and address customer pain. Proactive indicators help the business identify negative trends based on relatively small sample sizes—in other words, with limited customer impact. These techniques allow corrective actions to begin before a pervasive issue affecting a larger customer population is observed, allowing faster turnaround time on issues.

Customer experience metrics are used for the development of predictive indicators. Leading/predictive indicators rely on pre-shipment data to identify issues before customers experience them. Cause and effect are difficult to prove in most cases, but correlation analysis between this data and customer experience metrics, coupled with a good understanding of internal business processes, yields the best results. A successful predictive analytics program requires a very tight partnership between the business units and the corporate function defining the metric. Examples of these internal metrics are in-process indicators showing adoption of critical to quality practices.

Capturing customer expectations requires a deeper understanding of how customers intend to use the solution. The telecommunications industry classifies the network elements on the basis of their role or place in the network (PIN). Each PIN can be associated with a certain set of expectations—in terms of product quality, for example. Generalizing this concept to different industry segments can lead to segmentation of customers based on their expectations. If you can further quantify those expectations and measure performance (customer experience metrics) relative to them, you are going from minimizing pain into achieving customer delight.

Another consideration when looking at customer experience metrics is how to manage their proliferation. As you would track a metric for each customer touchpoint, the more touchpoints you have, the more metrics you need. The situation can get unwieldy if the number of touchpoints is large. It is important to create a layer of abstraction that simplifies management of the metrics without precluding "double-clicks" for additional details. A best practice here is to create indexes that serve as abstraction mechanisms for multiple metrics. You could also create heat maps that combine multiple indicators into a single visual representation. The heat map could guide decision makers to the areas that need attention while still providing a holistic view of the end-to-end customer life cycle.

Finally, telemetry data lends itself perfectly to be used for this category of metrics because it is collected at the point of contact between the customer and the system. This type of data promises to provide more real-time information (compared to existing customer experience sources) and enable the development of algorithm-based, self-correcting, adaptive experience systems.

3.4.3 Outcome Metrics

The final group measures customer outcomes from the inside-out and outside-in perspectives. These metrics can also be called *so what* metrics because they help in understanding if the pain measured in customer experience is actually getting in the way of the customer achieving his or her objectives and/or the organization meeting its financial goals:

- *Inside-out metrics.* These are internal indicators that help in understanding if solutions are delivering value to customers. Customers will stay away from solutions that provide limited or no value. You can monitor worsening trends on customer acquisition, customer losses, wallet share, and so forth, and use that as compelling evidence for customer-experience improvement action. When used at the right level of granularity, the balanced scorecard discussed previously can provide similar indications.

- *Outside-in metrics.* These are indicators used by customers to assess if products/services are delivering the desired value. They can be very diverse; however, they can be grouped into a few basic categories:
  — *Cost savings.* Is this product or service saving me money? The measure associated with this dimension saves money relative to some baseline expectation. If customers are not saving as much as they expected, then they are not satisfied. For example, a customer who buys a video-conferencing solution to save money on employee travel would want to measure "travel savings" over the life of the solution.
  — *Time savings.* Is this solution saving me time? The outcome metric associated with this is time reduction relative to some baseline. Time savings can be associated with increased productivity, which allows a customer operation to scale to higher throughput.
  — *Simplification.* Is this product removing complexity? This is an important consideration in a world where the speed of business continues to increase.

In addition to the preceding metrics, unstructured data plays a key role in driving a culture of quality and customer experience. For instance, top executives develop a strong sense of problematic trends in quality through their regular conversations with customers—even if they cannot quantify them. Unstructured data can serve as a source of anecdotal evidence that backs metric data in telling the story of what the customer is going through, thereby creating empathy. Also, in some cases, metric data acquisition can be difficult, and unstructured data can point clearly to what needs to be fixed. It is important—particularly in a strong culture of metric-based continuous improvement—that you prevent the absence of structured data from becoming an obstacle to driving improvement activities. In the final analysis, a healthy mix of both structured and unstructured data should always be sought when running the business of quality and customer experience.

3.5 CREATING A CLOSED LOOP FOR IMPROVING CUSTOMER EXPERIENCE

In this section, we go a step beyond the creation of insights and discuss what it takes to create a sustainable closed loop for improving the customer experience. We start our conversation by discussing the role of governance as a control system. From there, we talk about identification of key areas of focus, how to size the gaps, and bridging those gaps and sustaining the change. The outline and sequence of topics is listed here:

1. Setting up a governing body

2. Identification of key improvement areas

3. Cross-functional action teams

4. Gap analysis for key focus areas

5. Sustainability of improvements

6. Ongoing monitoring

3.5.1 Setting Up a Governing Body

A quality management policy or strategy cannot be realized without an effective governing body. The need for governance is less about employees intentionally sabotaging customer experiences and more about identifying and holding accountable those individuals or departments operating in misalignment with the stated strategy. Inconsistent organization priorities across functions are a typical source of gaps in the quality of the delivered data. Here are the key success factors for effective governance:

- Strong sponsorship directly from CEO

- Strong leadership that encourages debate but moves the discussion forward

- Cross-functional representation, ensuring critical departments are on the table

- Metrics that truly reflect customer experience

- Operational rigor, ensuring that actions are assigned and completed in a timely fashion and that consequences are enforced for inaction

Governance is one of those things that if overdone, creates more harm than good. Therefore, learning how to strike the right balance is very much an art. Case study 3.1 shows how governance plays a critical role in the way successful companies run their business.

Case Study 3.1: Governance in Action

In this case study, we review the role that governance plays in the running of a telecommunication service provider organization.

Introduction

A service provider is constantly altering its network infrastructure in order to provide services and keep up with customer needs and demands. The organization's success is directly tied to the health of its network. As a result, it is important to be diligent when network updates take place in order to minimize the chance that an infrastructure change may cause a service disruption. Regardless of whether there is preventive or corrective maintenance activity, implementation of additional capabilities, or introduction of new technology, there must be assurance that these activities will not cause unintended adverse effects on the customer's ability to run his or her business.

Governance is all about managing and protecting the infrastructure that customers are critically dependent upon. If implemented correctly, governance is not some bureaucratic process meant to slow real progress. It is not some process that demands producing documentation of little value or just an extra set of hoops to jump through. Governance is the common denominator of all successful operations.

Governance allows for tailoring the process to the activity being planned in order to streamline the time it takes for review and to limit the number of essential documents that provide the assurance that things are being done correctly. Governance should not be looked at as some adjunct activity, but rather as the way to do business. Introducing governance to the organization may be a change in the way things are currently done, but it is a healthy change that cannot be missed. This case study shows the benefits of implementing an industry-based governance process.

Benefits

The existence of an effective, well-defined governance process provides significant benefits to the organization and its internal and external customers. It offers a consistent process for developing, designing, and deploying infrastructure solutions.

A well-defined governance process assists in managing expectations and keeping governance boards focused and progressing toward common objectives. It helps to identify poor performing change requests early in the process so remedies can be constructed and applied before proceeding to the next phase.

For immature requests, governance provides a specific process for bringing them to an appropriate level of maturity for implementation. The presence of a well-defined governance process will contribute to the reduction in risk to the company and will lead to improved quality of service.

Another major benefit from a governance process is the decrease in lifecycle costs. Governance standardizes design and minimizes life-cycle costs associated with difficult-to-maintain solutions. The formal documentation required reduces maintenance by avoiding rework.

Additionally, those people maintaining the infrastructure can be more efficient by beginning with a complete and accurate set of procedural documents. A clearly defined governance process provides a consistent framework for operations and maintenance.

Frameworks

The need for a consistent governance process can never be overemphasized. The process ensures delivery of quality solutions while maintaining operational viability during the change. The governance structure must provide a mechanism to oversee a wide range of projects with diverse requirements, schedules, and resource needs, resulting in different levels of oversight. The establishment of a governance process involves, among other things, a good understanding of the assets, quick fixing of solutions, and a consistent action-tracking mechanism for changes.

Frameworks help bring uniformity, an ability to measure performance, and much-needed scientific rigor. Some of the more popular frameworks include the Capability Maturity Model Integrated (CMMI), Six Sigma, Control Objectives for Information and Related Technology (COBIT), and Information Technology Infrastructure Library (ITIL). Each framework has a particular area of emphasis. However, what sets ITIL apart is its strict focus on IT services and operations. When used properly, ITIL helps IT departments in all organizations—whether small or large and regardless of the sector—to improve their quality, including increased faster problem resolution and better security of the data.

The Central Computer and Telecommunications Agency, a now-defunct branch of the British government, first developed ITIL in the late 1980s as a catalog of best practices for government IT departments. Its use soon spread to the United Kingdom's private sector and then to European companies; over the past several years, it has made its way to the United States. Now in its third version, ITIL consists of more than 20 well-defined process disciplines that allow IT managers to improve the level of control that they have in their IT environments.

There are three key process disciplines that provide the most benefit if implemented at the onset of a governance process implementation. They are incident management, change management and configuration management.

Incident Management

The primary objective of incident management is to return a working solution to customers as quickly as possible. An *incident* is any event that is not part of the standard operation of a solution and that causes, or may cause, a nonconformance or reduction in the quality of that solution. All incidents are recorded, and the quality of the incident record determines the effectiveness of a number of other processes. Incident management helps to minimize the adverse impact of any solution on business operations, thus ensuring that the best possible levels of quality are maintained.

There should be a close interface between incident management and change management. If not properly controlled, changes may introduce new incidents. It is recommended that incident records be held in the same configuration management database (CMDB) as change records—or at least be linked without the need for rekeying—to control the nonconforming solutions.

The incident management process comprises the following activities:

- Incident detection and recording
- Incident classification and support
- Incident investigation and diagnosis
- Incident resolution and recovery
- Incident closure

At the heart of any well-run operation is change management. Therefore, if changes are controlled as soon as possible, the bulk of incidents will be prevented. This is definitely a quick win, and quick wins are good in order to keep the operations team motivated and upper management committed to a project.

Change Management

Change management is responsible for enabling beneficial changes to be made with minimum disruption to the solution. The change management plan (CMP) ensures that a common method is used to handle all proactive and reactive changes to the operational environment, including appropriate authorizations, planning, communications, scheduling, and evaluations. The implementation of this process ultimately leads to informed decisions and better understanding of the operational environment.

Proactive change is usually introduced to enable business benefits such as reducing costs, enhancing services, or increasing ease and effectiveness of support. *Reactive change* is introduced to resolve errors and adapt to changing circumstances.

What do all high-performing IT organizations have in common? They have a culture of change management that:

1. Prevents and deters unauthorized change
2. Utilizes "trust but verify" by using independent detective controls to reconcile production changes with authorized changes, ruling out change first in the repair cycle during outages
3. Utilizes lowest mean time to repair (MTTR)

Auditors will appreciate that in these high-performing IT organizations, change management is not viewed as bureaucratic but is, instead, the only safety net preventing them from becoming a low performer. In other words, IT management owns the controls to achieve its own business objectives—efficiently and effectively. Achieving a change success rate of greater than 70% is possible only with preventive and detective controls.

The CMP depends on the accuracy of the configuration data stored in the configuration management system (CMS) to ensure that the full impact of changes to the solution is known. Therefore, there is a very close relationship between configuration management and change management.

Configuration Management

Configuration management is responsible for maintaining information about configuration of the solution, including all parts and their relationships. Configuration management is the basis that helps to ensure that only authorized components are used in providing the solution. No organization can be fully efficient or effective unless it manages its solutions' assets well.

Configuration management is an integral part of traceability in the event that the solution has to be recalled. It allows for current, accurate, and comprehensive information about all components in the infrastructure to be stored in the CMDB, which in turn makes the management of change more effective and efficient. It is recommended that configuration management and change management be implemented simultaneously in order to maintain the integrity of the CMDB once it is first established as part of the configuration management process.

Because the CMDB stores relationships between an item that is to be changed and any other components of the solution, the owners of these components are allowed to be involved in the impact assessment process before a change is implemented. Whenever a change is made to the infrastructure of the solution, associated configuration management records should be updated in the CMDB. Where possible, this is best accomplished by using integrated tools that can automatically correlate changes to assets and other records.

The CMDB should be made available to the entire operations staff so that incidents can be resolved easily by understanding the possible cause of the failure. The CMDB should also be used to link the incident records to other appropriate records such as the failing configuration item (CI). An example of a CI would be a feature of a solution not providing outputs according to the requirement.

The configuration management process comprises the following activities:

- Management and planning

- Configuration identification

- Configuration control

- Status accounting and reporting

- Verification and audit

Conclusion

Governance discipline is required within an organization in order to reap the benefits of a well-run enterprise. Its implementation positively affects many parts of the enterprise, not just network operations. Processes, people, technology, and management will undergo a transformation that may require a new management structure, new technology, and changes to processes. Changing the technology alone will not be effective, and people will need to be trained on the new way of doing things. Although there will be many changes required to implement governance, the benefits surpass any inconveniences associated with adjusting the way things are currently done. Implementing governance is not an option but a requirement in order to achieve an effective and efficient operation of your business.

3.5.2 Identification of Key Improvement Areas

Identifying the right set of activities in terms of numbers and relevance that would have the greatest impact can be challenging. There is always more to do than time and resources allow. If you find yourself in this situation, the place to start is always with the customer. We need to use the combination of business knowledge and the direct and indirect voice of the customer to guide the decision-making process. Earlier in this chapter, we touched on customer feedback mechanisms typically used to collect the voice of the customer.

All of these are great sources of customer inputs. Once the data is gathered, analytics are applied to help identify the areas of focus. Leading organizations use Pareto analysis of customer support cases as a measure of where the customer pain exists. The higher-frequency items take the highest priority for action through improvement activities. The benefit of this approach is that you can readily see reductions in customer complaints as improvement activities are implemented and sustained.

Beyond data and analytics, the decision of which areas to focus on will require other considerations. Some of these include:

1. *Cost implications.* "Not all problems are created equal" and, therefore, what it takes to solve them can also differ greatly. Having a good return on investment analysis is a must when considering an improvement activity. However, the ability for the organization to undertake a costly rework can often get in the way.

   A common hurdle here is the lack of "quantifiable benefit" associated with quality improvement activities. Reduction in customer-found nonconformance does not easily translate to a clear revenue upside and/or an operational cost reduction, although the latter is much more manageable. In our experience, simple, consistent "conversion models" (e.g., converting nonconformance reduction to opportunity cost) are always preferred over complex models that are difficult to explain, understand, and get buy-in.

2. *Cross-functional ownership.* Unfortunately, not all customer experience improvement activities fall neatly within organizational boundaries. It is often the case that improvement activities require coordination/collaboration between multiple organizations or functions. Leading organizations tend to rely on corporate functions to settle, allocate, and mediate to solve a common customer issue. As we discussed previously, cross-functional governance provides the foundation for these types of decisions and transactions.

3. *Time implications.* Some problems are easier to solve than others. We typically refer to those as "low hanging fruit" due to the ease with which they

can be addressed. In a change management context, tackling easy problems during the early phases of the project can create a sense of progress and success that can motivate the team to tackle harder issues. Organizations break the harder problems into chunks that can be completed in a quarterly cadence. This allows teams to more accurately track the progress. Finally, it is important to consider the time to resolution in terms of the customer or market situation. There is always a certain type of problems that should not be solved internally because customers cannot wait for the solution and the market will move to some other alternative. This is particularly true in areas where the life expectancy of the solution is short compared to the time for solving the problem.

3.5.3 Cross-Functional Action Teams

How each functional department aligns and adds to the organization's strategy will obviously differ based on the role each department plays. However, a common success factor in how departments drive corrective actions is the inclusion of cross-functional members to ensure clarity of departmental needs and other departments' expectations. Successful organizations create multilevel governance to ensure clarity of decision making across large enterprises.

At the corporate level, decisions and operational tracking will be at a higher level of abstraction. However, the information is granular enough to ascertain status, and the accountability is clear enough to assign ownership for action. At the function level, decision and operational tracking will be at a level commensurate with the functional scope. The company-level abstractions of the metrics get reviewed at the corporate level by the CEO and his or her staff, where functional boards see renditions of the same metrics pertaining to the product or solution level.

As with the corporate governance board, functional boards need active engagement and sponsorship of functional leaders. There is no substitute for this. In the absence of leadership engagement, boards become "frustration-sharing" forums with little or no impact. Beyond leadership and common metrics, operational rigor is the next required ingredient for success. When metrics do not meet the preestablished goals, actions need to be assigned by the leaders with clear expectations of resolution time. A discipline of reviewing and tracking the status of assigned actions until resolution should be emphasized.

A perhaps nimbler model is the concept of combined product team (CPT). In this case, there is a centralized metric-generation team, but the improvement actions get assigned to a team that combines representation of the functions responsible for product life cycle, including support, development, and supply chain. The advantage of this approach is the simplicity and speed of execution. The challenge tends to be maintaining a consistent approach to driving improvement actions. This is not necessarily bad because cultural differences typically exist between product teams, and this approach better accommodates such differences.

3.5.4 Gap Analysis for Focus Areas

We highlighted the importance of segmentation in understanding customer expectations. When a segmentation model is extended to the way the company measures customer experience, it further improves time to resolution and, on occasion, the proactive identification of gaps. For example, a company delivering healthcare services to a segment of customers with high availability expectations should calibrate the definition of "preventive care" to match those expectations.

Another element is having a capability, known as a *listening team*, focused on capturing the voice of the customer. Care must be taken to ensure the intensity of listening efforts is consistent with the organization's ability and commitment to drive and consume the change. An overdriven listening effort that does not translate into visible results can actually become a source or amplifier of customer dissatisfaction. In fact, customers already feel that they are overly surveyed. For this reason, an approach that seeks to drive more action with information already at hand is the best.

Mature organizations realize that they already have, within the enterprise, sufficient information to triangulate and understand where the gaps are. They are creating data repositories (data lakes) where information from multiple internal sources is centralized. Thanks to advances in technology, these data lakes are "virtualized," meaning that information sources can still be dispersed across the enterprise but presented to users of the data lake as a single source. Focusing on tapping internal sources of information needs to be a main element of the company's next-generation listening strategy.

Beyond listening, an analytics capability helps mesh and correlate the voice of the customer with other structured and unstructured data, turning that data into actionable insights. These insights can be brought to the governance team to help drive action and decision making. In this situation, a typically overlooked role is the one of a storyteller. The detailed, step-by-step storyteller can translate data trends and metric status into a story that can be conveyed to internal audiences. The absence of a storytelling capability can significantly undermine analytical efforts. Insights will go unused because leaders lack the ability to translate these into terms that are relevant to their business.

Finally, as discussed earlier in this chapter, a strong measurement capability is required to keep the pulse of customer experience at the main points of the customer's life cycle. The information helps determine if corrective action needs to be undertaken or if ongoing actions are having the desired effect. Organizations define a common set of metrics that get reported at the corporate or functional level, depending on the audience. However, the ability to visualize these metrics through a simple dashboard and having the ability to "double-click" or drill-down for more detail is a success factor.

One suggestion is to avoid the unnecessary proliferation of metrics. When all is said and done, there should be no more than six quality metrics that get tracked and reported at the corporate level. A best practice here is to organize metrics into tiers (see Figure 3.6), where tier 1 metrics are the strategic indicators that your company is trying to affect. Tier 2 metrics allow for a double-click

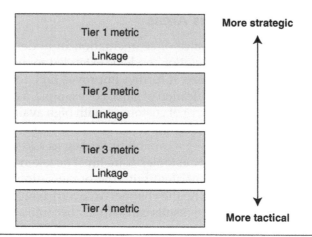

Figure 3.6   Hierarchy of metrics.

on tier 1 metrics. Tier 3 and 4 metrics can provide greater details and granularity. To have clear linkages between the tiers and an articulation of priority between them is critical.

3.5.5 Sustainability of Improvements

As customer experience improvement actions are identified and executed, care must be taken to ensure they are incorporated into the operational processes and tools of the company. This will ensure that improvements have the best chance of being sustained.

A continuous improvement loop needs to exist to ensure corrective actions are not only being applied on *what* is being delivered, but also on *how* things are being delivered.

There are four capabilities that need to be highlighted:

1. Process

2. Training

3. Tools

4. Communications

3.5.5.1 *Process*

"Process" refers to a set of interdependent activities required to achieve consistent results. As teams learn—whether from their own experience or from others—they utilize the process as the "container" to capture the lessons learned. An organization with a discipline of process definition and continual process improvement is likely to be characterized as a "learning" organization. The absence of process discipline typically leads to the opposite result with an organization that does not learn from its experiences.

Over the years, we have seen organizations that have been victimized by their lack of process discipline. The "p-word" (for *process*) is avoided at all cost. Employees will say: "Process just gets in the way; we want to make things happen." Employees are empowered to do "the right thing" and roam free from the shackles of process. At this point, an enterprise will begin to rely on staff as the keepers of institutional knowledge (IK). If you need help with a particular aspect of the work, you are referenced to individuals instead of knowledge portals. "Go talk to Jimmy, he will tell you how to best format the document" becomes a common phenomenon. While it is always true to some extent, total reliance on people for IK exposes the organization to lots of "relearning" as individuals move in and out of the organization. Even worse, as far as quality is concerned, is that processes critical to quality get forgotten and relearned. This translates to customer frustration, business risk, and additional costs.

While we are clearly not advocating for a burdensome process, we are convinced that process discipline—particularly around practices critical to quality—is indispensable. It will allow lessons from industry and personal experiences to be captured for future use.

3.5.5.2 *Training*

Just like process, training helps ensure lessons from the past are leveraged in the future. In the context of a quality management system (QMS), it is important to build focused training around critical-to-quality practices, quality policy, quality objectives, common quality metrics, and improvement action approaches. The advent of technologies like videos on demand allows scaling of training efforts and effortless sharing of best practices between and among individuals.

Successful delivery of defect-free, customer-centric solutions depends on employees with the appropriate qualifications, training, and skills. Roles also need to be well defined, and employees must understand their role and how their contributions impact the given solution, as well as the overall organization, in order for them to be productive and motivated.

As solution offerings evolve, roles, responsibilities, and proficiencies will evolve as well. The success of the business will depend, to a great measure, on the critical skills and expertise that employees have. In many organizations, employees are required to support multiple roles—that is, to wear many hats. For example, employees may be involved in the design of a solution, be asked to work on the implementation of the solution at a customer site, and then ultimately move into supporting the new or changed solution. Employees need to be cognizant of the role they are playing and be willing to support the role, even though they may feel more comfortable playing a different role. In order to help employees perform the role that has been assigned to them, role-specific training must be given that is relevant, practical, and useful. One of the methodologies for making training relevant and useful is to provide training as close to the launch of the solution as possible, which is also known as *just-in-time training*. This technique allows trained staff to have the training fresh in their mind when they start using or supporting the solution.

Training often gets relegated to the very end of a project because managers do not want it to "get in the way." But, similar to having a preference for a properly trained mechanic looking after our cars, we need to ensure we have only properly trained personnel supporting our customers. A well-documented, realistic training plan results in cost efficiencies that become a competitive differentiator.

Given the demand projects have on our schedules and the fact that people have different learning styles—such as visual, auditory, and kinesthetic—many organizations provide different training vehicles for employees to use based on their needs and time constraints. Some of the most common training vehicles used, include:

- *Instructor-led classroom training.* This training style involves an instructor and students in a contained room. Instructors deliver training in a lecture or classroom format as an interactive workshop. It involves demonstration with the opportunity for students to practice or virtually utilizes video-conferencing tools. Each student receives training documentation and has the opportunity to perform classroom exercises during the training session. A student guide is provided during classroom training to instruct individuals on the use of the solution and to perform a job procedure or skill. This guide will serve as a good reference once the student is back at his or her workplace.

- *Computer-based training (CBT).* This type of training allows employees to receive instruction whenever it is convenient, with short-use, case-based training modules accessible through the web. This self-paced delivery method grants 24/7 training access to geographically dispersed personnel, which then becomes part of a full learning library consisting of training modules and student guides that are available at any time for future reference.

- *On-the-job training (OJT).* This training style allows operations staff to reinforce what they learn during classroom training and/or CBT; it also provides an opportunity to ask questions in real time. OJT involves having training staff on site, where the job is being performed, to help with solution features.

To cement skills learned regardless of the training type being provided, a best practice is to provide hands-on training. This training provides students with the opportunity to use the new solution and conduct exercises in order to practice the instructions provided on the particular topic.

Approach to Training Development

Effective and efficient training needs to follow a well-structured and organized process with the following phases:

1. *Analysis.* The analysis phase involves the collection of information and analysis of requirements to evaluate the specifics that will be taught. It

includes understanding the task learner's need to perform, workflow, level of performance, learner audience, and objectives of training.

2. *Design.* The design phase focuses on setting realistic and measureable learning objectives. In addition, a plan for how training will flow and what content will be included is constructed. A major consideration is designing an instructional vehicle that includes real-life scenarios and exercises that simulate on-the-job mission experiences so the transfer of learning back to the job environment is maximized.

3. *Development.* The development phase involves structuring each of the courses. Content is created and assembled; interactive exercises are developed to simulate real-world, on-the-job conditions; and quizzes or questions are constructed to measure attendee understanding. Training content modules are reviewed and revised according to feedback.

4. *Implementation.* The implementation phase is responsible for ensuring files necessary to launch the training are successfully uploaded and the learning application or website is functional. The learner takes the training and assessments are administered.

5. *Evaluation.* This phase is the backbone of the training approach. At the end of the training session, students are given an opportunity to evaluate the course and the learning experience on ease of use, navigation, course content, exercises, and effectiveness of training. Survey data and metrics are used to improve courses as needed. The analysis of the data allows for continual improvement of training materials to better ensure the training efficiency and effectiveness.

3.5.5.3 *Tools*

Tools play many roles in the quality management system, and they are important in the specific context of training for at least two reasons: knowledge capture and automation.

Knowledge Capture

In previous sections, we spoke about the importance of having process discipline to capture lessons from experience (yours and industry). There are tools called "workflow tools" that can be leveraged as containers of these lessons. A success factor is the ability to keep them updated with the latest lessons learned. A perfect illustration of this type of tools is a tax preparation tool. The tool "knows" the tax code (in the United States) and keeps up with changes year over year. As a user, you can follow a consistent process of entering your tax-relevant information, and the tool applies the appropriate rules based on latest "tax knowledge."

Organizations that have a weak process discipline can build a strong dependency on tools as a "workaround." While you still are better off having both process discipline and workflow tools, having a strong tools culture helps you to retain institutional lessons if these lessons are instantiated in the tools.

Automation

Today's urgent demand for solutions that can be supplied with a high level of quality requires automation. The importance of automation cannot be downplayed because it helps in reducing waste, costs associated with production, and lead times. It has brought significant advantages not only in the manufacturing world, but also in the service and software worlds, and it has given a new flexibility to organizations in the redevelopment and redesign of their products. Along with other benefits, it has helped in increasing:

- Productivity

- Safety

- Speed of doing overall business

- Consistency of execution

Clearly, automation via tools allows rapid execution of tasks or reproduction of solutions. However, it is the ability to create consistency of execution that makes automation relevant. When you learn about a nonconformance that escaped your automated process, you can modify the automation to account for it. Again, automation enables continuous improvement and sustainability of lessons.

Case Study 3.2: Automation in Action: Profile-Based Software Testing

This case study provides an example of how automation is used by organizations to drive sustainable improvements in customer experience. It shows the entire process adhered to by an organization that builds embedded software for its solutions and validates the software with automated tools.

Today, many software development organizations have extensive automation test facilities to allow them to consistently and expeditiously validate new software against their customers' operational profiles. These facilities are a critical element of their solution-delivery process, and they invest significant resources in development and maintenance. Depending on the solution, advances in technologies allow for physical separation between the physical equipment (e.g., the lab) and the individuals designing and conducting the verification (e.g., an individual conducting a pilot).

The development of the profile-based automation system involves the following steps:

1. *Profile creation.* On the front end of the process, designated individuals work with customers and field employees to painstakingly capture whether the customer is from a large or small organization, as well as the customer's usage patterns of the solution. These patterns are known as *customer profiles* and are generally created for customers who generate top revenue.

2. *Profile implementation.* The profiles then get aggregated and built into solutions and associated training. This step is complex because customers are very different by nature, and their usage of the solutions also differs. Therefore, aggregation of incorrect patterns will defeat the purpose of profile-based validation.

3. *Use case creation.* At this point, we are ready to begin capturing operational scenarios that represent the dynamics of customer usage. Scenarios that represent the following situations, among others, are created:
   — How do you conduct maintenance in your solutions?
   — How do you handle nonconformance isolation?
   — How do you deal with associated feature, security, or
     data vulnerabilities?

4. *Validation of solution.* With the use cases, you can begin validating the solution. Sequencing of cases, capture of results, and handling of nonconforming conditions are some of the end results.

5. *Execution.* Now, it is a matter of identifying the outputs against the original requirements. Troubleshooting skills become critical because you need to discern the difference between identifying nonconformity and identifying a problem with the validation skills and efforts.

6. *Post-execution assessment.* Shortly after completion of the validation, the team will get together to capture what went well and what can be improved in the software. This assessment should include identifying nonconformances that made it to customers and figuring how to prevent them from escaping again, as well as issues identified during validation.

3.5.5.4 *Communications*

Storytelling is a key capability for change management. Communication helps ensure consistency of messages, regular cadence, and clear calls to action. Those with experience in people management or leadership will resonate with the importance of having clarity of purpose and coherence of message. Individuals at the receiving end can get confused or numb to the barrages of information. For this reason, leveraging communication specialists in the area of quality management will make the difference between a successful and an ineffective improvement action.

It is ideal to create a communication plan that describes:

- *What.* Objective you want to accomplish with your communications

- *How.* How can the objectives be accomplished, including defining appropriate tools

- *Who.* The audience to whom your communications will be addressed

- *When.* Timing and sequence

- *Impact.* Measuring the results of the communication plan

Communications will include all written, spoken, and electronic interactions with the target audience. These may include, but not be limited to:

- Digital signage
- Committee and board communiqués
- Printed publications
- Online communications
- E-mail signatures
- Legal and legislative documents
- Voice mail messages
- Corporate identity materials, including special badge, letterhead, logo, and envelopes
- Employee surveys
- Certificates and awards

3.5.6 Ongoing Monitoring

It is no secret that even well-run organizations can become victims to disruptive changes in the market. A strong tracking of customer expectations tied with good situational awareness of the market is a good recipe for success. The ability to anticipate market fluctuations provides you with the necessary time to retool and adapt. Also, setting clear expectations with employees for continuous change and improvement is necessary. A robust continuing education program with tight alignment to the strategy will increase the odds of success and reduce the time to adapt or retool.

"Disrupt or get disrupted" seems to be the basic premise in business today. We see how business innovation seems to be trumping solution innovation. This shift allows a faster speed of change in the business that is less constrained by solution development life cycles. Those who know what is happening within the organization, the industry, and the world are able to keep a finger on the global pulse and are in a better position to anticipate trends that may affect their industry.

3.6 IMPROVING CUSTOMER EXPERIENCE THROUGH INTENTIONAL DESIGN

In previous sections, we discussed how customer experience and insights can be used to drive continuing improvement activities with solutions. However, there is another value proposition for customer experience and insights that is inherently more proactive and impactful. It starts with the realization that more than simply focusing on capturing the experience, we need to understand—and even influence—customer expectations. The promise of customer expectations is that they allow us to intentionally design solutions that meet those expectations from the start.

At first glance, understanding customer expectations may seem like a daunting task. How do we do that? As a colleague once said to me, "Can we simply ask the customer?" As it turns out, mature organizations have been doing this for a while and, for the most part, without ever asking their customers. Particularly as it relates to next-generation solutions, what customers "experienced" in the previous generation represents a good approximation of what they "expect" from the next one. Thus, organizations that design solutions with customer expectations in mind have an advantage. It is particularly relevant in situations where you have different teams developing each generation of solutions and these teams are in different organizations or even countries.

Sometimes, expectations change dramatically from one solution generation to the next. These changes might have little to do with the experience of current-generation solutions but, rather, are transitions in business model, competition, operational profiles, or regulations. Therefore, having a good procedure for regularly calibrating customer expectations is required. A best practice is using customer-facing employees as a key source of customer expectation information. They can identify what matters the most and changes in the customer "care-abouts."

In addition to collecting customer expectation data, a new pipeline needs to be created to feed the information to the right place inside the organization (see Figure 3.7). Solution managers are responsible for developing the solution requirements with feedback from customers, salespersons, and other relevant interested parties. Therefore, these solution and project managers shape design decisions and need to understand the latest state of customer expectations. Some organizations have a process to insert customer expectation into the workflow of the solution managers. The idea is that as new solutions or features are defined in their workflow tools, customer expectations of reliability, usability, and so forth, automatically become embedded in the design of the features. At the same time, lessons learned from customer experience such as nonconformance and issues with configuration (among other issues) are also

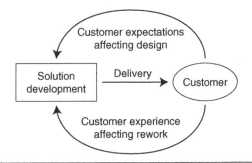

Figure 3.7   Customer experience versus customer expectations.

considered when new solutions are designed and developed. This helps in eliminating the same types of problems from creeping up again.

Leading companies are in the midst of digitizing their operating processes. As a critical step in this journey, leaders are looking to democratize (free up) data that currently exist trapped in multiple functional silos. In order to bust the silos, data scientists have developed the capability to interweave customer information across multiple databases without necessarily making them compliant with master data foundation standards. Some of the capabilities in place today are the ability to look at three or four large databases and identify records associated with the same customer or the same solution across the databases. This development is expected to significantly expand the impact of customer experience already within the walls of the enterprise.

Also, enterprises should never feel they are hopelessly subject to the whims of customers; they can absolutely "influence" customer expectations. There are many ways to shape customer expectations, including marketing, competition, adjacent markets experience, current experience, etc. Organizations that can successfully influence customer expectations can create market differentiation and competitive advantage.

Some would argue you should not be designing new products based on customer requirements at all! Steve Jobs was famously quoted as saying, "You can't just ask customers what they want and then try to give that to them. By the time you get it built, they'll want something new." Likewise, Henry Ford said, "If I had asked people what they wanted, they would have said faster horses."[23] What both of these leaders clearly share is the view that transformational ideas do not always come from existing users. People tend to think incrementally from an existing idea versus reimagining a whole new solution. Apple has built a successful business model out of creating markets with new products and ideas—basically, as Jobs said, showing customers what they need. Nevertheless, this approach does not work well in every situation. It works best in emerging markets where customer expectations have not yet been set or influenced by existing solutions.

3.7 ADAPTIVE CUSTOMER EXPERIENCE THROUGH TELEMETRY DATA

Today, most of the data used to measure customer experience come from analysis of customer calls. Customer call data (volume, resolution code, product association) typically get processed once a month, at which point, downstream metrics based on it are updated. Depending on the metric, a statistically significant change in trends will not raise an alert until it happens for at least two reporting cycles (two months) in a row. So, at this point, we are at least two months lagging from the moment the customer experienced the pain that triggered the call.

Additionally, due to the metric normalization (e.g., install base) applied to remove noise, a small (relative to total population) number of issues keep the metric from moving outside of its control range. Analogous to turning a large ship compared with a small boat, strategic metrics won't move unless a significant portion of the install base experiences a problem. So again, this set of customer calls will not trigger a systemic corrective action until the problem becomes more pervasive.

It is fair to say that it would be preferable to assess customer experience with data collected *before* a customer calls to complain and to do so with sufficient granularity to detect outliers. Telemetry data is collected by the system in real time while it is up, running, and interacting with its users (or paying customers). So, telemetry-based data promise a new class of customer experience metrics and associated insights that more accurately represent customer pain.

Additionally, telemetry data can enable machine-learning algorithms that would react to real-time changing conditions. These algorithms will "live" inside the system itself and would have the ability to be tuned or parameterized. This capability would definitely usher in a new era in customer experience similar to the self-healing network mechanisms of the past. We refer to this era as the *adaptive customer experience*.

Adaptive customer experience may sound like futuristic stuff; however, it is very much within our grasp today. As mentioned earlier, one of the authors of this book is a runner, and part of his running gear is a watch that tracks his distance, pace, heart rate, etc., in real time. Because he is still relatively new to running, he uses his watch to help him get the most endurance out of his current physical condition. When he goes out for a run, he relies on the watch to tell him his pulse (heart rate) and pace in real time. Not wanting to run the heart rate too high and burn out, he throttles his pace to keep the heart rate in a good zone. This approach allows him to adapt running to what his body (heart rate) is saying. While, in this case, his brain is providing the closed loop, you can envision a time where applications would exist that combine both of these data streams, apply some analytics, and guide a runner through vocal commands to the desired pace based on a prespecified configuration.

If the technology is available, what is getting in the way of companies developing telemetry-based customer experience metrics and moving toward adaptive customer experience? Leading companies are already working on this. "Born-in-the-cloud" companies are used to supporting customers in a different way. They utilize continuous development methodologies that blur the line between development of software and customer support. These companies are perhaps in the best position to begin capitalizing on telemetry data to incorporate new customer experience metrics and the integration of algorithms that would lead to adaptive experience.

However, not all is lost for traditional companies that were not born in the cloud. What is needed is a different collaborative mindset between development and support engineers to mimic the ideal of continuous development. Development engineers need to tap the experience of support engineers to figure what aspects of the customer life cycle should be metricized using telemetry. Then both teams need to work in partnership with data scientists to develop and tune machine-learning algorithms that can bring adaptive customer experience to life.

NOTES

1. Definition of word "data": *Oxford Dictionaries.com* (Oxford University Press, July 2017).

2. A very brief history of pure mathematics: *The Ishango Bone*, University of Western Australia, School of Mathematics, http://www.maths.uwa.edu.au /~schultz/3M3/history.html (retrieved January 2007).

3. Bernard Marr, "A brief history of big data everyone should read," World Economic Forum Agenda, 2015.

4. Richard Millar Devens, *Encyclopedia of Commercial and Business Anecdotes* (New York: D. Appleton and Company, 1865).

5. René Cassin, "Pascal tercentenary celebration," *Nature* (1942).

6. N. Krevans, "Callimachus and the pedestrian muse: Callimachus II," *Hellenistica Groningana 7: Callimachus II* (Leuven, Belgium: 2004), p. 173.

7. P. J. Parson, "Libraries," in *Oxford Classical Dictionary*, 3rd ed. (Cambridge: Oxford University Press, 1996).

8. Heather A. Phillips, "The Great Library of Alexandria?" *Library Philosophy and Practice*, August 2010.

9. "The Pinakes," http://www.grece.org (retrieved May 29, 2010).

10. Paul E. Black, ed., Entry for "data structure" in *Dictionary of Algorithms and Data Structures*, online version (U.S. National Institute of Standards and Technology, December 15, 2004).

11. Carey, Wodehouse, "SQL vs. NoSQL Databases: What's the Difference?" https://www.upwork.com/hiring/data/sql-vs-nosql-databases-whats -the-difference (retrieved February 13, 2018).

12. "Jepsen: MongoDB stale reads," *Aphyr.com*, May 20, 2015, retrieved March 6, 2017.

13. "Large volume data analysis on the Typesafe Reactive Platform," *Slideshare .net* (retrieved March 6, 2017).

14. Adam Fowler, "10 NoSQL misconceptions," *Dummies.com*, retrieved March 6, 2017.

15. "NoSQL relational database management system: Home page," *Strozzi.it*, October 2, 2007, retrieved March 29, 2010.

16. "NoSQL 2009," *Blog.sym-link.com*, May 12, 2009, retrieved March 29, 2010.

17. Douglas Laney, "3D management: Controlling data volume, velocity and variety, " Gartner, February 6, 2001.

18. V. Dhar, "Data science and prediction," *Communications of the ACM* 56, no. 12 (2013), p. 64. doi:10.1145/2500499; Jeff Leek, "The key word in 'data science' is not data, it is science," *Simply Statistics*, December 12, 2013.

19. Thomas H. Davenport and D. J. Patil, "Data scientist: The sexiest job of the 21st century," *Harvard Business Review*, October 2012.

20. James Manyika, Michael Chui, Brad Brown, Jacques Bughin, Richard Dobbs, Charles Roxburgh, and Angela Hung Byers, "Big data: The next frontier for innovation, competition, and productivity," McKinsey & Company, May 2011.

21. Doug Henschen, "Big data analytics master's degrees: 20 top programs," *Information Week*, January 7, 2013.

22. Eric Blattberg, "NY gets new bootcamp for data scientists: It's free, but harder to get into than Harvard," *Venture Beat*, April 15, 2014.

23. Patrick Vlaskovits, "Henry Ford, innovation, and that 'faster horse' quote," *Harvard Business Review*, August 29, 2011.

4

Telemetry and Customer Success

In this chapter, we will review how telemetry can be used to create a software development organization that is more responsive and efficient at meeting customer needs, starting with a review of the traditional requirement traceability approaches. We will discuss how to build a software development organization that is telemetry enabled, the concept of data threading in the context of telemetry, how to build a telemetry infrastructure, how to prepare the data to make it easy-to-consume within the organization, and how the customer success model is perfectly tailored to take advantage of telemetry data to derive increased business value. To explain these concepts, the chapter is organized into the following sections:

1. Tracing requirements to finished product

2. Designing a telemetry-enabled organization

3. Data handling and data models in telemetry

4. Data threading in telemetry

5. Telemetry infrastructure

6. Telemetry feedback loop

7. Data preparation steps

8. Customer success

4.1 TRACING REQUIREMENTS TO FINISHED PRODUCT

Understanding how specific customer asks are traced to the final delivered product is often a mystery for many in the software profession. Unlike traditional manufacturing, a single requirement may originate from multiple sources. Adding to this, complexity in the organizational structure creates opportunities for multiple interpretations, which may eventually result in missing requirement traceability or misinterpreted asks. Though many in the industry would not publicly acknowledge it, there are many developed software features/capabilities that are either rarely used or not used at all by customers.

In a typical software-centric product development company, the time from requirement defined to delivery can range from three to six months. In case of a hardware-centric product, this cycle can be much longer, typically ranging from 12 to 18 months. Considering the workforce is comprised primarily of knowledge workers and not preprogrammed robots, keeping workers coordinated throughout the development cycle can feel more like an art than a science.

However, it is evident that the closer knit the development teams are and the shorter the delivery times, the more relevant the outcomes are to customers. These observations may feel obvious to those operating in startup companies, but achieving the same can be daunting in an established midsize or large firm trying to disrupt the market with the next big idea.

In this chapter, we show how telemetry—and, more specifically, a telemetry-enabled product development effort—can help bring about more relevant customer outcomes. We will do so by diving into the nuances of the requirement-to-delivery cycle and show how a lack of rigor (or scientific approach) brings down the overall efficiency of the organization. For a modern digital company, the lack of requirement visibility and traceability means a business failure in the long run.

4.1.1 Requirements Gathering—Beginning of a Broken Pipeline

A requirement (or request) can be seen as the true embryo (or essence) for an end product. This essence needs to be preserved throughout the life cycle of the product in order to deliver the intended value. Unfortunately, the essence can be easily lost or distorted at any point. Losing the essence is not desirable in a product development environment; to prevent that, requirement documents were born. How detailed these documents need to be has been debated with every new development methodology that has emerged over the years; however, they all have agreed that these requirements need to be clear and the essence needs to be preserved. Monolithic requirement documents, sometimes called the business requirement documents (BRDs), are slowly giving way to shorter Agile-based user stories (Agile is a well-known industry standard software development method and the work breakdown is done by splitting the overall requirements into small chunks of work known as user stories). These shorter documents, while still adhering to the original principles, leave many things unclear. Without any first-hand inputs from the customer to supplement these documents, the essence tends to get diluted or outright lost.

In this important first phase of product creation, such discrepancies can be the beginning of the end. Without careful control, an ask for a "classy product" can easily become a "glassy product" at the end of the supply chain (one that looks good but does not meet quality standards). If this happens, the downstream phases of development seldom loop back to recheck the actual request, and hence, this may become a point of no return in many cases.

If the startup culture is studied in depth, its success can be easily attributed to probably just one factor: feedback. As the number of handoffs is low (given the smaller size of the organization), the chance of a requirement veering off course is greatly minimized. Action on feedback—in the form of a new require-ment or a bug fix—greatly enhances the chances of success for this fledging organization. Revenue growth, unfortunately, almost always comes at the cost of the agility that a startup company thrives on.

Can a large or midsize organization reduce these inherited inefficiencies? This question involving process improvement and value analysis is asked at regular intervals by management teams in big companies. These exercises involve commissioning an external consultant who faithfully delivers a book-let full of fancy graphics to explain what may be improved. However, even before this exercise is done, the answer is probably known by everyone in the company but seldom articulated. The answer, which is generally uncomfort-able, is usually attributed to the overhead in the system, which in turn is prob-ably the result of inefficient management. The fear of recrimination leads to denial and lethargy in changing the environment. This is a dangerous spiral, where the company will continue to churn out unusable products, leading to customer and market dissatisfaction.

4.1.2 Software Development as a Traditional Production Line

Manufacturing processes (primarily hardware) have evolved over many years. Their benchmark of improvement had always been the trifecta of cost, quality, and time. The software industry, which is relatively nascent, also set benchmarks like its old-school manufacturing counterparts. Software meth-odology soon evolved to achieve these benchmarks. Terms were intermixed and derived acronyms were produced. This approach did work, albeit briefly, during the days with many investors and very few ideas to develop. As the saying goes, all things that go up must come down, and this happened to the software industry as well. Multiple recessions, bubble bursts, and downturns shook the industry and made companies rethink their operating models. This self-introspection took them back to "rediscover" the importance of the trifecta: cost, quality, and time.

Inventory management, lean production, and cost optimization all find their roots in classical manufacturing. Industries thrived or perished depend-ing on how they cut costs without compromising on quality—all done before anyone else moves ahead. The market leaders broke away from competition even though all players seem to doing similar things. Their success can be attributed to a concept called *organizational visibility*. This visibility allowed suc-cessful companies to identify mistakes, correct them, and move ahead, all in a relatively quick time frame and with minimal financial damage. Does this sound familiar to the behavior of today's startup?

Though the manufacturing principles were time tested, the software industry realized these needed to be amended to satisfy current needs. It was understood that the assembly-line principles that applied to manufacturing a television or a car could not be applied to producing working software. How-ever, the development discipline and visibility present in a product line needed to be retained in the software environment. However, this self-realization does not definitely mean everyone acted accordingly, and like everything else in life, actual implementation is what matters most.

Now let us take a step back and look at quality. Foremost, quality can be construed as the bridge between the delivered product and the original ask or requirement. This requirement, however, rarely translates directly to any functional or product term. And herein lies the smartness of the organization to pick on the subtle cues and build to solve that ask. Have you heard the axiom, "The business exists because of the customer requirement"? When cars were invented, "the ask" was probably to have something that allowed faster commuting that was more comfortable than horse carriages. It was surely not something that said ". . . burn gasoline and provide a lot of thrust. . . ." It is also to be noted, though, that the originally delivered product solved the basic need before anything else. Fancy chassis and multi-injected cylinders came later.

Particularly in mid- and large-scale enterprises, the software industry—with its large profit margins—provided room for inefficiencies to thrive and, shockingly, be accepted. What is considered acceptable quality has been particularly subject to the whims and fancies of all related and unrelated parties. With the lever of quality being so easy to compromise, more immediate and lucrative metrics, like cost, took precedence.

There is another important facet of a requirement too. It is not explicitly said, but it is mostly implied. In the example of a car, it is almost a given that the vehicle would have good fuel efficiency, comfortable seating, agreeable emission levels, etc. These unstated requirements are sometimes referred to as nonfunctional requirements (NFRs). Now let's get back to today's reality of the software industry. We have already discussed how quality being an implicit reflection of the requirement is so easy diluted. NFRs are interpreted differently throughout the developments phases, too. In fact, related requests such as security, performance, and ease of use are interpreted differently by different layers in the organization, with the lack of clearly written expectations. Considering that software development is a distributed operation containing various silos, the lack of adherence to quality and delivering something close to the requirement gets more challenging.

In the final analysis, it is the lack of a common vision or understanding of the big picture that is the biggest limiting factor in achieving engagement from the knowledge workers. Solving this is easier said than done because components of the product are developed across cultures, time zones, and charters. The lowest-level developer seldom is apprised of the bigger picture and his or her contribution to it. This mindset, probably borrowed from the manufacturing world, is not optimal for a knowledge worker who relies primarily on creativity rather than defined steps to solve a problem. Apart from stifling the freedom to do exploratory coding, there is a real financial risk related to integration as well. With silos working on a requirement that was already diluted, there is a real and almost inevitable risk of failure when the integration takes place. Again, statistically, it has been proven that integration is one of the major points of failure in a software project. If, in spite of all the gaps in understanding, a project does get delivered, maintenance and serviceability will surely become the Achilles' heel for the product and may soon turn out to be a liability for the company.

We hope the importance of creating a common golden thread from customer requirements and, most importantly, keeping this thread intact during the development process is now clear. The traceability of any code being written back to its original requirement is arguably the most important attribute for a successful software development program.

In our earlier example of car or TV production lines on a manufacturing floor, every component and every inventory is accounted for and measured for cost, quality, availability, and usage. Excess and obsolete material is considered inefficient and treated as a priority for correction on an ongoing basis. Every unit produced is accounted for and tracked until the quote-to-cash cycle is completed. In summary, nothing goes unnoticed in a factory floor and on a production line. Missing a production target and timeline is not acceptable, and repeated failures can result in closure of the production line and, eventually, closure of the factory. Every serial number is tracked, and every component is counted and is traceable during the life cycle of a product. Quality and time sensitivity are well rewarded. Deviation from the original requirement will result in rejection of the end product. In the end, no one escapes the quality and traceability cycle of the production line.

In contrast, consider a software development life cycle. Missing requirements and missing timelines are lesser sins and often accepted as part of the life cycle. Quality is not a prime concern for most software engineers. Writing a piece of software that somehow works is the first priority. Scalability, performance, serviceability, and security aspects are seldom considered during the initial cycles of development. Questions like the following must be the primary concern of any responsible engineer: How far can software scale when it is put into production? How many users can it support in addition to concurrent transactions with the load factor applied? How well can it troubleshoot an issue? How secure is the software? Unfortunately, such questions are typically of little concern for many modern-day developers. It is very easy for a car to be recalled from the market if any of its core functionalities (like air bags) are missing, but somehow it is not seen as a serious issue in the software world.

The situation in software gets further complicated when multisite and multicultural developers come together to contribute to the same piece of code. Everyone adds his or her part of the logic to the code, and in the end, it somehow works! But no individual knows the system end to end when it comes to traceability or troubleshooting. During the process of code development, the original customer request gets buried in detail and often forgotten until the time of release. Integrating and testing code written by several different players and testing takes a considerable portion of the total development cycle. The real user of the product and the developers rarely meet, if at all. Because the code is written by several individuals with very loosely coupled connections and relationships, it is extremely difficult for any individual in the process to understand the life cycle of the product from beginning to end. How customers use the product is not a prime concern for development engineers, and they will move to the next project after the coding project is completed. The build (also known as compiling and bundling the software together) and delivery of the shippable software is done by another department. Therefore, unlike a factory floor, the software development life cycle is often associated with high costs and inefficiencies.

As seen in the following illustration, a software life cycle is still not a straightforward undertaking. The current industry is widely divided between those adopting Agile versus those using Waterfall, and this adds more complexity to the already full pipeline of requirement tracking and prioritization. Not only is the industry divided, but the engineering and program management functions within the same company—and sometimes under the same leadership—are also divided. Leadership, in many cases, is not willing to take a firm stand because many leaders have the mindset of waterfall but were forced or persuaded to embrace the agile mindset. While our intention is not to look at the people aspect of agile or waterfall methodologies, it is important to look at the damage this debate is creating across the industry in terms of process inefficiencies, eventually creating a confused state of affairs between the original requester of the functionalities and the developer of the product.

Any approach that can provide structure to implement requirement-to-delivery traceability will be a game changer. In the next few sections, we review the basic building blocks of end-to-end traceability while pointing out the key elements of a successful implementation. Before we do that, let's first look at a traditional software development workflow, which is not designed to adhere to the traceability expectations.

Figure 4.1 is a generalized view of organizations that are struggling with tool hopping (going through multiple tools), multiple standards, and lack of traceability, leading to a one-directional flow of information that eventually results in a nontraceable work product. It is a standard representation of how a mid- to large-scale company operates, but it may not be representative of startup or small-scale firms.

The classical software life cycle has five distinct phases:

1. *Gather.* This phase indicates requirement gathering and prioritization of those requirements. Typical personas involved here are product managers and technical marketing engineers. These personas are usually part of sales or marketing organizations and minimally connected to the engineering functions that actually work on those requirements. Lack of standard process and workflow can create the first level of disconnect.

2. *Plan.* In this phase, people and resources are added to the project, and it is then handed over to the engineering department. Personas involved here are program managers, product engineers, development managers, test managers, and a few process-level planners. In a traditional process flow, the requirements prioritized in the gather phase are handed over via electronic documents like e-mail or spreadsheets, but they may not have the proper traceability. There is no common standard process which the software industry adheres to in this phase; it is surprising to see that even

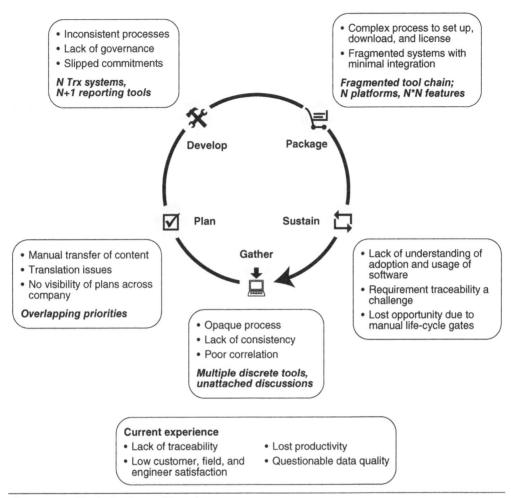

Figure 4.1 Classical software life cycle.

large-scale enterprises still handle this phase via e-mails and spreadsheets with no backward or forward traceability.

3. *Develop.* This phase is focused on software and hardware engineers and the processes associated with such personnel. Various agile tools (e.g., Jira, Rally, Target process) are used depending on the agile coach hired, and the same organization may have all of these tools coexist. The issue we have seen in this phase is the complete lack of high-level visibility of what is getting done and what is being dropped. There are reporting mechanisms available with each of these methods, but they seldom provide a traceable view of what portion of requirements is missing from the big picture. If agile implementations are that alarming, we can only imagine the issues associated with waterfall!

4. *Package and release.* In this phase, the primary personas are regression testers, integrations testers, build engineers, release program managers,

and product managers. This is where the licenses are embedded in the software and systems. This is also the place where software and hardware are packaged together to form the bundle for sale. This is the most crucial phase for the telemetry-based design because the packaging can often determine if the system can track the usage by license probes and because telemetry probes can be inserted into the licensing bundle. It is very likely that this domain is very busy and is bustling with numerous players working together to release the product. Lack of automation and process is usually a common scenario and can destroy the operational effectiveness. Another issue we have witnessed in this domain is the presence of very complex, large, and distributed systems. A software build-farm, which is an array of hardware combined together to provide processing power, can spread across the world and can take several hours to compile a version of code. Similarly, code reviews, static analysis, commitment workflows, and associated process can make the build process extremely tedious to troubleshoot and can inject errors and faults that can break the entire flow of data traceability.

5. *Sustain.* This is where the actual usage of the software product occurs and data gathering for future improvement happens. If the previous phases are well done, this phase will be uneventful. If we miss the traceability aspects in the earlier phases, this can be the most challenging phase of all! It is here that data can be a real friend, providing valuable insights like usage patterns and renewal opportunities. The majority of current systems are not developed with embedded telemetry or traceability. While the industry pundits may call it Internet of Things (IoT), for the software-embedded product developer, this is where telemetry of the system comes to life.

4.2 DESIGNING A TELEMETRY-ENABLED ORGANIZATION

In order for an organization to successfully transform itself to respond effectively to telemetry data, it has to realign and exhibit certain characteristics. Listed here are the five characteristics that demonstrate an organization is ready to adopt telemetry-enabled product development design:

1. Clear personas or roles

2. Feedback loops

3. Workflow and rule engines

4. Reporting and analytics

5. Data awareness design and data modeling

4.2.1 Clear Personas

An organization is a collection of individuals and teams who are marching toward a common goal. Clear demarcation of roles is necessary to facilitate the smooth functioning of a large collection of individuals. These boundaries must eliminate gray areas and provide a clear purpose to the value chain.

The responsibility may loosely tie to job titles or functions in an organization. The roles and responsibilities can be associated with an individual or a bunch of individuals. Typical roles within a development organization can be product marketing, development, testing, program management, release engineering, and so forth. For successful execution, these roles have to be mapped into a flow.

Let's step back, and look into the workings of a typical organization. If you look at the delivery mechanism holistically, it is nothing but a synchronized process of interactions between and among roles. If this synchronization is clear and there are no gray areas in terms of responsibility, between the roles, you are ready to realize the complete benefits of telemetry. It is recommended these roles—or *personas*—be built (through digitization) into the operating model of the organization. This is more robust, considering the fluid nature of the workforce in the industry. Digitizing also fulfills the need for accountability with audits and compliance documentation.

To summarize, to achieve a true telemetry-enabled architecture, the processes and architecture must clearly connect the interactions of the different personas.

4.2.2 Feedback Loops

A telemetry-ready system must be designed to accept and act on feedback. Feedback can be both manual and automatic. The latter is gaining great strides with the advent of IoT and related technologies. In previous constructs, feedback was limited to communication between people. With the advent of networks, this grew, to an extent, to include automated e-mails and selected notifications, but the scope of feedback was still very limited. As connectivity became the norm, information exchange took a gigantic leap forward, and the concept of tracking all details became a possibility. This massive information exchange can be realized without any added effort.

Businesses and products have to be equipped to both receive this data and then translate any incoming data into useful metrics. If the interpersonal and process connections are in place, this metric will be vital for process improvement. Such proactive processes produce products that are the closest to the customer needs. A responsive development system is possible, but only if this is built into the product design from day one. Adding this capability after the fact is inefficient and time consuming.

4.2.3 Workflow and Rule Engines

Interactions between people and process need to be controlled and orchestrated. This is possible by digitizing the process using workflow and rule engines. Employing these mechanisms enables the organization to track bottlenecks and trace the requirement end to end. This visibility is invaluable in creating effective value chains and reducing waste. Again, these throttles need to be built into the design, rather than retrofitted later, to get the best results.

4.2.4 Reporting and Analytics

What good is all the data, if it is not used? An organization needs to build in capabilities to clean, sort, thread, aggregate, and make sense of the data. "If you torture the data long enough, it will confess to anything," said Darrell Huff in *How to Lie with Statistics*.[1] It is imperative to ask the right questions of the data and gather the right insights. It is also important for the data system to get the correct answers within a reasonable amount of time. Various big data technologies are widely available that enable very flexible architectures to facilitate this. We discuss designing a correct reporting system in detail in Chapter 5.

4.2.5 Data Awareness Design and Modeling

A telemetry-enabled organization becomes the custodian of a large amount of data. A plan needs to be in place to handle this huge volume of data. Technology becomes just one aspect of this management. Associated checks pertaining to data security, data sovereignty, and legality need to be factored in, too. Another aspect is how well organized this data is. The more organized, the easier it is to thread and make sense of the data. The hardware and database design need to support scalability and performance, which would be expected of the insights coming out of this data.

Intelligence is directly proportional to the number of data points. For companies to be relevant with intelligence, they have to deal with massive volumes of data and process and make sense of them within a very short period of time to retain market position. In this chapter, we look into effective means of designing responsive data repositories to host data.

Not all data is created equal, and hence, all data should not be treated with the same priority. Classification is necessary to come up with strategies regarding security, data privacy, data retention, and data storage. Data can be broadly classified as two major types from a telemetry point of view:

• Master data

• Transactional data

With the influx of modern software languages and ready-made libraries that are easily and freely available on the internet, the software industry is witnessing an emerging new challenge. "Cut-and-paste" programmers, who are in their mid-twenties with an eagerness and mindset for rapid prototyping, are quickly becoming the norm. The long-term impact for such short-sighted coding approaches will only be known when the system is put into production and subjected to load and performance conditions. One of the scariest consequences of this practice is turning the entire software industry into a playground for cyberattackers. Universities are not helping either because most modern software engineering curricula seldom focus on quality, performance, scalability, serviceability, or security-based programming practices. Instead, most of the focus is on software libraries and application program interfaces (APIs).

When all is said and done, the most critical element of a telemetry-enabled organization is the data and how it is moved from source to destination with well-threaded streams. Let's look at some data fundamentals and their usage in creating a modern traceability framework, focusing only on the data from a traceability perspective and how we plan to use such data in our design.

4.2.5.1 *Master Data*

Master data has the following characteristics:

- Changes minimally over time

- Used as a reference across functions

- Used as look-up data for validation

- Forms the basis for aggregation and segmentation

This type of data is important to set goal posts for aggregation and decision making. The contents of this data have a commonly known definition across the company. Maintaining this collection is very important for large enterprises—where common protocols and yardsticks are of the utmost importance—in their efforts to compare and act on important cross-functional decisions.

Information of this magnitude has far-reaching consequences in analytics and decision making. Hence, this data has to be highly governed and protected. As this data can also contain confidential information, it has to be highly secured. The use and scope of such data must be designed into the initial data architecture for any enterprise application and must not be done as an afterthought.

Apart from commonly used master data, organizations can demark their own special data sets to fall in this category. Some of the most common collections are:

- Customer definitions

- Product definitions and hierarchy

- Partner information

- Spare parts catalog

- Fiscal calendar

The contents of these collections are fed in manually, through aggregations over time or publicly available reference data sets such as holiday lists, time zones, country/state information, and the like. The intent of this book is not to go deeply into any of these terms, as each of them can easily be a subject for several days of reading. It is our recommendation that any serious developer who wants to do an enterprise-level software design should understand these subjects well.

4.2.5.2 *Transactional Data*

Transactional data is constantly touched and churned. These data points vary from a few seconds (as in a stock market quote) to short bursts (like blood sugar levels from an IoT device). This data needs an infrastructure that supports this constant change.

In technical terms, the complete incoming information needs to be verified for consistency, completeness, and authenticity before recording the transaction. Both the recording but also the retrieval of this data must be fast and accurate. This may seem like a small request, but the complexity required to achieve it becomes massive as the flow of data grows. The system design needs to account for this data growth and put an infrastructure in place that can be easily scaled on demand. If this step is missed, teams will end up spending a lot of time later doing data migrations and transpositions, adding unnecessary development cycles. We will look into the availability of existing technologies to facilitate this requirement in a later section.

There is also a subset of transactional data referred to as "reporting ready." Using raw transactional data in reports is not required in most cases because businesses primarily look for outliers. Exceptions are provided in the form of aggregations. The need for stakeholders to access raw data must be carefully scrutinized to avoid an unnecessary load in an already strained infrastructure that is handling the transactional data. Some examples include:

1. *Raw materials/products in enterprise resource planning (ERP).* Data pertaining to components, parts, and licenses that are part of the product mix and that are usually compared with ERP data sets

2. *Customer.* Data originating from a customer network and/or mapped to a specific customer

3. *Partner.* Data originating from a partner network that can provide a rich set of usage patterns, which are usually not possible from a customer network

There are other master data and transactional data examples available in the industry, and a simple internet search can provide more details.

4.3 DATA HANDLING AND DATA MODELS IN TELEMETRY

4.3.1 Collection of Data

Before starting to collect, we must address:

• How will the data be used, and what are the associated benefits?

• What are you going to measure, and how it will impact the business?

We must start by understanding the kinds of usage patterns and correlation expectations arising from the data. We have a two-model approach: one that focuses on core attributes and common rollups and another that focuses on rich data sets that store all information for eventual use.

You must develop a value proposition for each of the data entities being collected from telemetry, both from a customer and an organizational benefit point of view. There are several aspects we need to keep under consideration while collecting the data. In a telemetry world, data collection needs the highest level of technical and infrastructure planning and an extreme level of sophistication because the incoming volume can be enormous. Archival policies, offline storage, intermediate storage, etc., need to be considered while designing this data system. A section in Chapter 5 discusses this in more detail and recommends the designs best suited for large-scale telemetry data gathering.

4.3.2 Minimum Data Set

The minimum data set includes the core attributes that describe and help in further aggregating information flowing in from various end points. As an example, the minimum data set for telemetry of a product should provide and collect information from the product that will allow us to track whether a customer is on the ideal adoption journey toward his or her desired outcome and, if not, help determine what intervention is necessary. Some examples for understanding this better are:

- Customer information

- Device registration information

- Device health information

- Feature utilization

- Application events

- Application logs

Methods for the collection of data need to be designed at the time of architecting the software. There should be probes and provisions embedded in the software to do it. Once the software is developed, it is a tedious task to insert these probes into the system, which can then result in serious performance degradation and often introduce security vulnerabilities. Identifying minimum data sets and patterns from the huge incoming volume is a high-skill task and requires a deep understanding of the domain and the product.

4.3.3 Privacy and Security

Your attention to a well-defined hierarchy of entitlements that drive access and authorization will be helpful. Well-thought-out sensitivity models and results would have a higher security rating, while the rich, unprocessed data can be more democratized for a wider audience to explore and recommend. Subscription-based models can be designed to achieve event-based notifications using streaming solutions such as KAFKA and FLUME. Data classification per security standards needs to be done and certified by the information security organization, and a role-based access (RBAC) mechanism needs to be implemented to meet current requirements.

Another facet of safety is related to the end point itself. Because it allows an entry point into the enterprise network, the end point needs to be well secured with latest malware/ransomware detection and prevention methods. Consider the case of a router that is deployed at a customer's location. If we are collecting telemetry data from that device, we can call it our end-point device. Having built-in security within the device and securing the ports and network pipeline are very important aspects of the telemetry design. Data, once taken out, must be transported over a highly secured pipeline to make sure that no leakage occurs along the way because such data could contain crucial information. In addition, because each device has built-in intelligence to carry out specific actions, remote management of these devices has to be again very closely secured and monitored.

Telemetry and traceability data often contain fundamental information. The highest level of safety should be enabled at each stage of the data processing chain. This data should be protected as highly classified and not allowed to be modified under any circumstances. People involved in handling this data must be highly skilled and well trained in the relevant domains.

4.4 DATA THREADING FOR TELEMETRY

We will now walk you through a few important aspects in the software life cycle where data and data threading play a serious role. It is critical to look at how a standard product development organization works and how the process flows with feedback and without a feedback loop. Telemetry and feedback loops are not accidents but parameters intentionally designed from the start. In other words, telemetry is not an afterthought but a necessary design ingredient.

While requirements could originate from any source inside or outside the company, for the ease of understanding the concept, let us assume the requirement is originated from a customer:

> *Example:* A requirement is given to a product marketing engineer through an e-mail or written document. The product marketing engineering uses the internal collaboration system to store the requirement for further processing, such as requirement prioritization, ranking, and portfolio management.

In this example, the internal collaboration system represents the first level of data threading, where we need to establish the master data and consider this as the single source of truth (SSOT). This is a critical step in any life cycle to identify the source of truth and protect it from any unauthorized change. Most software engineers do not track this step effectively. Requirements are often stored in spreadsheets and offline mechanisms, typically staying as an e-mail attachment, which can be lost in transition or disappearing when the product engineer leaves the company or changes teams.

During the second level of data threading, we need to elaborate on the hand-off from product marketing engineers to the portfolio team. While this may sound like a non-Agile step for many modern developers, this is the missing link that most Agile teams struggle to identify. The process of resource allocation and funding for a requirement to be engineered is a mystery for many of today's software developers. It is a problem with those using an Agile-based method as well as for those using a waterfall approach. The engineering handoff requirement should not be a soft handoff, particularly for projects that need strict quality and cost management. In order to avoid this, each requirement should be identified and connected to a portfolio item to track in terms of time, money, and quality. While we can call this step a concept commitment, it is often missed by Agile teams as well. It is a mandatory step for designing an end-to-end traceable system.

The third level of data threading is the handoff from the portfolio systems team to engineering development. Because these are, typically, two different teams, the chances of data connectivity loss and broken traceability are very high. Generally, the systems used in portfolio management are different from those used in development, and they are not designed to talk to each other. Your due diligence in data threading should be based on the interconnectivity design. How an original ask gets translated to a feature and how a requester can view what's happening within the development world is crucial—again, the data layer is the key. Agile development practices claim to address this problem by storing the entire set of requirements in the form of user stories, but in practice, with product development efforts spanning multiple teams and geographical regions, they will still struggle to have a meaningful solution to traceability regardless of using Agile or waterfall.

Finally, once the product is ready to be released to customers, the internal engineering and product marketing teams need to get feedback. Feedback in the form of case logs or support calls seldom provide meaningful insights or real analysis. Telemetry provides the best opportunity for obtaining data on customer usage and customer behavior. Both of these can be tracked through careful data gathering and data threading. It is paramount that the underlying infrastructure and data design are capable of supporting such massive incoming data sets.

We will illustrate the preceding points through two simple graphics that show the traditional software life cycle with and without built-in traceability. Then, the technical and architectural components necessary for building such a system can be explained. There are several technology solutions that can be used for data mining and data representation; however, we focus on the basic system and data threading design in this chapter. In the next chapter, we explain some of building blocks and potential technology choices for such systems in detail.

Figure 4.2 shows the process flow of a system designed with a one-directional flow of data and information as we have experienced in the typical usage of waterfall life cycle. As shown in the figure, the requirement often

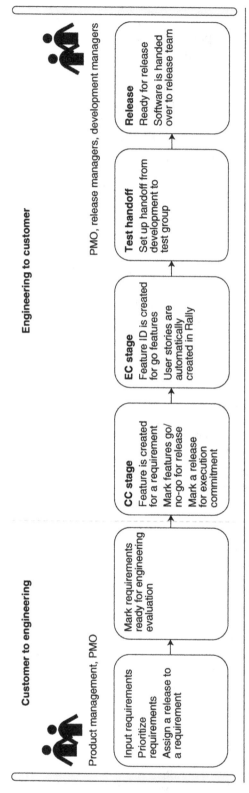

Customer to engineering

Product management, PMO

Engineering to customer

PMO, release managers, development managers

Input requirements
Prioritize requirements
Assign a release to a requirement

Mark requirements ready for engineering evaluation

CC stage
Feature is created for a requirement
Mark features go/no-go for release
Mark a release for execution commitment

EC stage
Feature ID is created for go features
User stories are automatically created in Rally

Test handoff
Set up handoff from development to test group

Release
Ready for release
Software is handed over to release team

Figure 4.2 Customer-to-customer life cycle.

initiates from a customer and flow to the requirement-gathering system for prioritization. The direction of the arrows shows the one-directional relationship between various stages in the life cycle, which is precisely the problem we want to highlight. As the data leaves the requirement phase and proceeds to the portfolio and concept commitment phase, the personas involved will change, as well as the underlying systems and data models. As we proceed further down into the development and testing cycle, we again change people, processes, and the underlying system. At every stage, there is a high chance of traceability being lost, and thereby, we end up with a broken pipeline. By the time the software reaches the customer, it must have gone through four to five hand-offs as well as any number of different systems and data models. Anyone familiar with data threading and system design can imagine the amount of information lost in this process.

Although Agile partially addresses early development feedback by keeping a closed loop with customer, it often does not address traceability once the product is out of development and ready for release. Collecting the customer feedback and threading it back to the prioritization cycle creates robust traceability.

Product telemetry is gaining popularity as the vehicle for requirement traceability. More and more product companies are now depending on telemetry to learn about usage patterns, product behavior, and potential customer sentiments. For engineers and planners, telemetry feedback is a vehicle for designing a better system based on actual customer usage that, otherwise, they would have no access to.

The building blocks of a telemetry-based product system are shown in Figure 4.3. As illustrated, the feedback data flowing from customer end points and getting collected by the aggregator are essential input back to the development process. Instrumenting a feedback loop in the programming plus a well-threaded underlying data model can create a closed-loop development system. Each stage of the process is connected forward and backward through these workflow architectures.

4.5 TELEMETRY INFRASTRUCTURE

It is imperative that there be a consistent mechanism to collect telemetry data with references tags that are well understood. Most of the activity with respect to telemetry takes place after the information is collected:

- Analysis
- Aggregation
- Patterns and co-relations

The above-mentioned elements are made possible only with a data architecture that drives the need for consistency in collecting information. The architecture to collect information doesn't need to be unified because each end point would

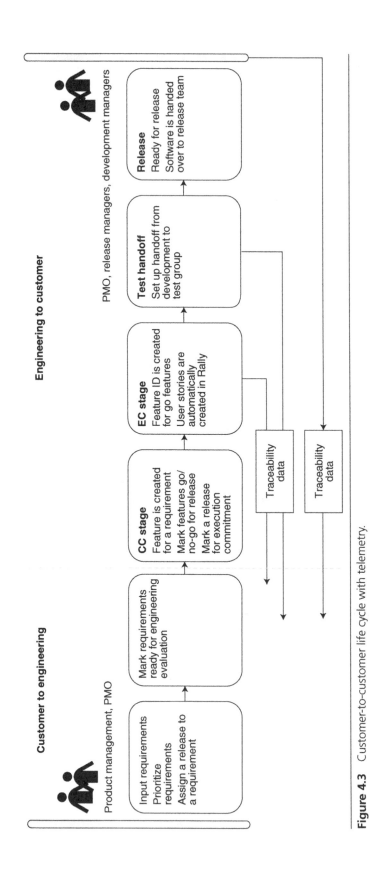

Figure 4.3 Customer-to-customer life cycle with telemetry.

have its own characteristics, but it is important to have a standardized information capture.

Having a common telemetry framework will help to:

- Improve maintainability

- Ease product onboarding process

- Set up standard security implementation

- Obtain better data control

- Ensure data resides in one place

- Achieve a single stop for data catalog

For example, assume there are three products: product A sends telemetry for feature usage, entitlement, and customer information; product B sends just entitlement and customer information; and product C sends just entitlement data. Because these products did not follow a common telemetry architecture to gather data, you will not achieve a good product insight on common parameters.

Therefore, having a common architecture is very important for collecting the telemetry data, processing that data, and generating the report/insights. Product companies that have several products can leverage telemetry to collect data/metrics from each product and store them in a common place for further processing or insight generation.

4.5.1 End-Device Data Threading

There are various methods available to collect data from end devices. The end devices themselves can be different in each case. But before getting into the modes and techniques for collecting data from the end points, it is necessary to define the two categories of telemetry data: hardware-based telemetry and software-based telemetry. In the next two sections, we will briefly examine these types in some detail. As the IoT grows, we will encounter more varieties of end devices.

4.5.1.1 *Hardware-Based Telemetry*

If your objective is to find system- and board-level information, then you are probably using hardware telemetry. In this case, the instrumentation is done through system- and board-level insertion, and the signals coming out of this instrumentation are usually in binary format. This type of telemetry can help detect assembly and printed circuit board assembly (PCBA)–level faults. These include (but are not limited to) noise levels, bandwidth degradation, and heat conditions on a board. This type of data is used for system monitoring, fault injection, and detection.

4.5.1.2 *Software-Based Telemetry*

Software-based telemetry, on the other hand, is code-level instrumentation and part of the software loaded on specific hardware. There are very specific code flows and usage information that can be monitored. In most cases, deriving customer data will depend on industry and regulatory policies/standards.

4.5.2 Types of Telemetry End Points

There are several types of end devices used for telemetry data collection. Generally, these systems can be classified as either: on-premise (OnPrem) devices or cloud-hosted (software as a service [SaaS]) devices).

4.5.2.1 On-Premise Devices

The OnPrem concept involves using the physical device present in the customer location and connected to the wide-area network (WAN). On-premise devices will be under the supervision or administrative domain of the customer. In this case, the incoming telemetry data will contain customer usage patterns, and the probes are usually built into the device software.

4.5.2.2 SaaS-Based End Points

In SaaS-based telemetry, the cloud-hosted software will have telemetry probes. End devices in this case will not have any specific hard-coded probes or agents for telemetry collection. With the influx of cloud-based hosting technology, SaaS-based models are gaining prominence. For ease of understanding the concept, a SaaS infrastructure allows centralized software management of all remote devices from a single point. Life-cycle activities such as software download, patches, upgrades, and licensing distribution are all managed centrally from the cloud, and the end device is just a plug-and-play entity (relatively dumb). For the purposes of telemetry in the SaaS model, there is a central point of telemetry data collection as well. While it sounds simple, the approach is still evolving with several standards and developments in process to address any remaining technical challenges. In this case, the cloud can be seen as a centrally hosted infrastructure that is highly secured, highly available, and accessible over a high-speed network. In the SaaS-based model, data access is controlled by the cloud service provider and not by the end user.

4.5.3 Probes and Collectors

Once you are able to insert a probe into the edge or SaaS end point, the next step is the edge data collector or telemetry aggregator. An edge data collector is the last-mile device or the first entry point of data from the collector. In the case of hardware-based telemetry, the edge collector will be a decoder that can interpret binary information. For software-based telemetry, the aggregator will be a policy-based orchestration engine with inbound data collection listeners. In other words, these are agents within the centralized listening software that can be activated to "listen" for incoming data streams and redirect them to a centralized data repository.

4.5.4 Telemetry Considerations

The next few components of the telemetry system are going to be internal to your company. Depending on the internal IT infrastructure and design, the system can include:

- A storage cloud

- Ingestion points

- A data analyzer

- A caching system

- Machine-learning systems

- A visualization layer and an API layer for a feedback loop into the engineering systems

Each of these above areas will be explained in detail as part of our reference architecture in the next chapter. For now, let's consider these as the various components of the reference architecture that, together, form a successful telemetry system. First stop in the system is a storage cloud, which is simply a place to land all the incoming data for further processing. Most of this will be raw data with no formatting or massaging. Then, the ingestion points are the entry points into the cloud that are considered the ports of data entry into the core telemetry system. The caching system and data analyzer will process the data for specific usage and predictions. Once analyzed, data will be subject to further processing through machine-learning algorithms and artificial intelligence processes performing deep inspection. Usually these steps are handled by data scientists and/or specialized data experts. Finally, insight and analytics are presented through front-end systems (or dashboards) and can be integrated into the engineering workflow via feedback APIs (application program interfaces).

It is important to note that any data collection and/or activation of telemetry probes in on-premise devices is strictly under the discretion of the end customer. In many instances, the main obstacle to implementing a telemetry system is the customer's unwillingness to activate the probes. Sales and marketing teams need to be specially trained to include this consideration during the sales process because obtaining access to customer usage pattern and customer sentiments will better enable the telemetry system. In our view, customers should be incentivized for such access, and the analytics/findings should be shared with them. As an example, if the customer purchases 10 features and activated all of them, feedback about how each of these features is used will be equally beneficial to both parties. The customer can make use of this information to make a decision during the next renewal cycle or to buy another product. The software company can use this information to decide if it is necessary to provide additional usage-based incentives. Also, the engineering team can use the information to prioritize development efforts and bug fixes.

Figure 4.4 provides a high-level overview of a telemetry system.

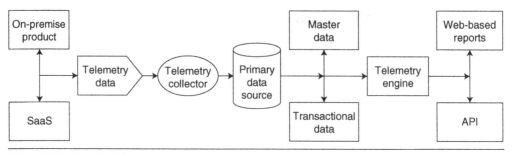

Figure 4.4 Generic telemetry ecosystem.

4.6 TELEMETRY DATA AND THE FEEDBACK LOOP

Before starting to collect, you should think about how the data will be used and the associated benefits. Also, you should think about what you are going to measure and how it will impact the business and the customer experience. In order to create use cases in the software application/tools, you will need input data. The input data is very important for each use case. This data is used to generate the output/report. Examples of data generators include sensor flows, event modeling, conditional notifications, active enquiries, etc. These can be collected through data ingestion patterns: HTTP (representational state transfer [REST]–based message transfer, which is built based on a transmission control protocol [TCP] stack where the end devices can communicate directly based on request/response mode), MQTT (message queue telemetry transport, which is a device-to-device communication mechanism that involves a broker as a mediator with two end devices based in publish/subscribe mode), AMQP (advanced message queuing protocol, which is an open standard for passing business messages between applications on different business entities), and Edge Analytics/ETL (extract, transform, and load, which is a term used for pulling data out of source systems and loading it into a centralized data warehouse).

Sensor flows are signals generated from sensors across the network, and they are periodically collected by an aggregator unit. These signals are not processed at the edge devices. Only relevant information is passed upward from the aggregator unit to avoid unnecessary network traffic. Event modeling is a method to trigger notification based on a system-critical event. This could be a fan failure or a CPU hog or a memory failure. Conditional notification are event-based notifications that are preconfigured to act based on a trigger set by the administrator. This allows monitoring vital parameters and making crucial decisions in the event of a system threshold event. Active inquiries are the ones initiated by the telemetry administrator to gather information at any given time based on the need.

Data generated by products on the customer's premise needs to be collected into a central database. There are multiple ways to do this, such as using a cloud-based collector from a cloud service provider like Amazon Web Service (AWS) or any other cloud-based storage service where data will be stored for a short duration. From here, it can be pulled into a big data platform, which will form the central database. This cloud-based collection needs to be secured both ways and must always remain on.

Connectors will be responsible for connecting between products and cloud-based collectors. Products must be able to support the connector without affecting its performance. Any telemetry data collection or push/pull mechanism can be used. Whenever the data is generated in the product, it should be transferred to a remote database by using message brokers. Examples would be KAFKA/RabbitMQ, two queuing and scheduling open-source software options often used in a workflow and orchestration environment. Although there are traditional queuing mechanisms like Informatica and shell scripting, more and more developers are using these modern queuing technologies.

4.6.1 Controller

Formatting is based on the centralized policies and processes that need to be applied to the collected data. Data collected would vary depending on each device/end point. There needs to be a subset-based collation for common data sets with reference to the extended rich dataset that has the complete information. Collected data could be aggregated in the cloud collector and published in a serialized format based on a product type, like the AVRO format. AVRO is an open-source standard that allows big data exchange with platform or language agnostic format.

Further, when data is pulled into a centralized database, it could be stored by segregating it based on the columnar family of that product type and stored in a big data platform (using a standard such as MapReduce, technically referred to as MapR). Using this approach, product data with different telemetry fields/schemas could be all stored in a centralized database using a different columnar family.

4.7 DATA PREPARATION STEPS

The following data preparation steps make it easier to start leveraging data from a telemetry-based system:

- *Data analysis.* The data is audited for errors and anomalies that need to be corrected. For large data sets, data preparation applications prove helpful in producing metadata and uncovering problems.

- *Creating an intuitive workflow.* A workflow consisting of a sequence of data preparation operations for addressing the data errors is then formulated.

- *Validation.* The correctness of the workflow is evaluated against a representative sample of the dataset. This process may call for adjustments to the workflow when previously undetected errors are found.

- *Transformation.* Once you are convinced of the effectiveness of the workflow, transformation may now be carried out, and the actual data preparation process takes place.

- *Backflow of cleaned data.* Finally, steps must also be taken for the clean data to replace the original, uncleaned data sources.

Finally, one should take note that each of these steps requires deep technical knowledge given the complexity of the data under consideration and also the sheer volume of data involved. Telemetry is a subject to be handled by an expert who is highly skilled in this type of activity. While we tried to simplify the steps to create a basic understanding of the concepts involved, the complexity involved and the need for careful planning cannot be overstated.

4.8 CUSTOMER SUCCESS

The customer success model[2] is a good example of a business model that takes advantage of, and heavily relies on, telemetry data. This model is most commonly used in the software world and is most prevalent among software as a service (SaaS) companies.

Customer success is about customers receiving the value they expect when investing in a vendor's product or service. It seeks to drive an ongoing conversation between vendors and customers to determine goals and make sure the solutions provided help them achieve their business outcomes. As illustrated in Figure 4.5, customer success seeks to address the ever-increasing complexity gap between the functionality delivered in software solutions and the value that customers derive from those solutions.

Customer success fundamentally changes the traditional sales model, as illustrated in Figure 4.6. In the traditional sales model, you have roles like account manager, channel partner, and service representative. All of these players are compensated via sales commissions or sales quotas. Thus, they are motivated to get customers to buy, regardless of whether the solution is really what the customer needs to solve his or her business objectives.

On the other hand, customer success teaches sales employees that closing the sale is only the beginning of a journey that includes getting customers to

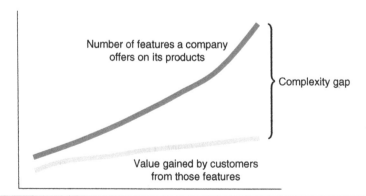

Figure 4.5 Why customer success matters.

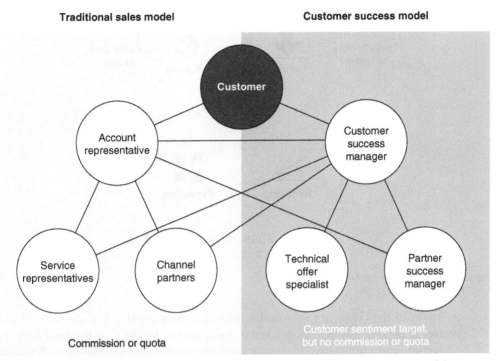

Figure 4.6 Difference between the traditional sales model and the customer success model.

adopt what they bought and remove any barriers affecting their realization of value. So, equivalent sales roles include customer success manager, partner success manager, and technical offer specialist. All of these players tend to be compensated on the basis of a customer sentiment target (e.g., Net Promoter Score™) and not on the basis of a sales quota. This fundamental change drives a different behavior wherein both customer and vendor are focused on finding the right solutions to the customer's business problems.

In the customer success model, the customer life cycle has four distinct phases (as illustrated in Figure 4.7):

1. Landing

2. Adopting

3. Expanding

4. Renewing

Let's review each of these phases in a little more detail.

4.8.1 Landing

The landing phase of the customer success life cycle entails getting customers to actually "buy" the product or service. However, unlike the traditional sales model, where the vendor receives full payment for the product or service,

Fast and easy deployment — Landing | Adopting — Faster time to value

Customer success

Frictionless — Renewing | Expanding — Let's do more

Focus on maintaining customer engagement throughout the life cycle

Figure 4.7 Customer success life cycle.

in this case the customer is actually buying a subscription (or service). In this phase, it is very important to have a good understanding of the problem the customer is trying to solve to ensure the service offered addresses that. It would be a disservice to the customer or the vendor to convince the customer to buy a subscription to a capability that they don't really need.

4.8.2 Adopting

In the adopting phase, the focus is on ensuring the customer is adopting (or using) the capabilities he or she purchased in the landing phase. Telemetry data plays a critical role in informing the customer and vendor alike of what capabilities are actually being used. For those that are not being used, an analysis needs to be conducted to understand what is getting in the way of adoption. Possible outcomes of this analysis include:

- *Customer needs training.* Feature is useful, but the customer does not know how to use it.

- *Customer is not aware.* The feature might be useful, but the customer is not aware it is there. A good example of this is a person who subscribes to the Amazon Prime service to get faster and (perhaps) cheaper delivery times but may not be aware of other capabilities (like video) that come included with the service.

- *Customer does not need the feature.* The customer is aware and knows how to use the feature, but simply does not need it.

- *Feature does not work.* There may be a quality issue, or the feature does not provide the intended value as designed.

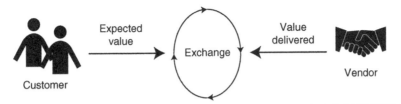

Figure 4.8   Customer success value exchange.

4.8.3 Expanding

In the expanding phase, the customer decides to add capabilities to their original subscription services. Clearly, if customers are not satisfied with value exchange, they will need to add capabilities to their subscription. So, once again, ensuring that customers only buy what they really need and are using what they paid for is a prerequisite for success in this phase. Telemetry data can be used to provide the necessary evidence to demonstrate value.

4.8.4 Renewing

In the renewing phase, vendors harvest what they sow. If customers are satisfied with the value exchange, they will likely renew and continue the business relationship. If not, this is the end of the road.

Summarizing, the widespread adoption of customer success powered by telemetry data has the potential of transforming (for the better) the relationship between customers and suppliers. As illustrated in Figure 4.8, the focus on the value exchange will naturally drive an increase in relevance, quality, and time to market. Vendors will no longer be trying to develop 100 features in the hope that customers use 30, but will, instead, develop the right 30 features from the beginning.

This chapter focused on the basics of how the development team's structure and processes influence the ability of an organization to design and implement telemetry-based system. The principles and viewpoints shared throughout the chapter are from our real-life experience (practice and observations) across many product development environments and projects.

NOTES

1. Darrell Huff, *How to Lie with Statistics* (New York: W. W. Norton, 1993). "If you torture the data long enough, it will confess to anything," July 17, 2017. *Wiktionary, The Free Dictionary*. Retrieved January 22, 2018, from https://en .wiktionary.org/w/index.php?title=if_you_torture_the_data_long _enough,_it_will_confess_to_anything&oldid=47041588.

2. Forrester Research, "An executive primer to customer success management," April 2014.

5

Required Telemetry Discipline

In the previous chapter, we discussed how to go about creating a software development organization that is most responsive to customer needs using telemetry data. We referred to those teams as "telemetry-enabled organizations." In this chapter, we focus on the skills and capabilities needed to build and sustain such a team. We will also review various technology options in the market that can be leveraged to realize a telemetry infrastructure and accelerate the workforce transformation.

As shown in Figure 5.1, a basic telemetry-enabled ecosystem is comprised of two primary players: the customer and the vendor. Both of these players face similar questions as they embark on the telemetry journey. However, the answers and the approaches to answering these questions will differ significantly between them and require different skills.

The Customer

- *Why:* Reasons for collecting or allowing the vendor to collect its data

- *How:* How the data will be collected

Figure 5.1 Customer and business telemetry considerations.

- *When:* The schedule and frequency of data collection

- *What:* What type of data needs to be collected by the customer or the vendor

The Vendor

- *Why:* To clearly articulate the business objectives for collecting customer data

- *How:* How the data will be collected in order to preserve the integrity, security, and privacy

- *When:* The frequency with which the data should be collected in order to make them actionable

- *What:* What will be done with the data and the type of actions that vendor will pursue

Both of these players need staff with the appropriate skills to answer these questions and help create a sustainable work environment. In this chapter, we will focus on the following areas:

1. Change management

2. Data ownership

3. Technology options for telemetry infrastructure

4. Customer onboarding

5. Policy and governance

6. Telemetry ecosystem stakeholders

7. Telemetry legal framework and potential risks

8. Bringing it all together: The art and science of telemetry design

5.1 CHANGE MANAGEMENT

Hiring talent from outside for driving your telemetry program is not always advisable or practical. Creating telemetry-enabled products is the result of deep-rooted domain knowledge. So, the best way to create the foundation for a telemetry system is to systemically and deliberately build a team with the right skills over a period of time. A common misnomer is that all you need for a telemetry-enabled organization is a few data scientists. The implication is that data science is the one skill needed to make telemetry a reality. In fact, telemetry and data science are often mentioned together and sometimes mistaken for one another. However, in reality, data science and data scientists are just one of many components in a telemetry system.

As you build your telemetry team, you must keep the following considerations in mind:

- You must approach this transformation as a cultural change

- Everyone must be onboard, accepting and fully aware of the new way of collecting customer data

- You must understand the implications for existing systems and technology

- You must understand how this information will impact/change existing business practices

- Everyone must be made aware of data protection and security implications and responsibilities

5.1.1 Cultural Change

Cultural change is a key consideration as you drive your telemetry transformation. A simple assessment within an organization for the number of leaders aware of the telemetry concept could be a good starting point for an organizational redesign. While figuring out what leaders are aware of in terms of telemetry is a good start, what you are really aiming for is an understanding of how many leaders and change agents already exist in the organization who know what it takes to build a telemetry system and what should be done with the data. Our observation is that only a small number of leaders are really aware of the impact and influence of telemetry-based designs.

To build a culture of telemetry, the organization—at all levels—needs to understand the processes required for smooth functioning of the system. Management must know the long-term impact on the business, and engineers must have/maintain deep knowledge of the technical and architectural elements of telemetry-based designs.

Shifting convictions and processes to support data-driven development is perhaps the toughest aspect of the change. You will have to enlist a change agent at the executive level who can explicitly communicate the purpose of telemetry and its benefits. Because executive leadership sets the company culture, they are in the best possible position to ensure all concerns associated with the change are addressed and any potential roadblocks removed.

5.1.2 Everyone On Board

The outcomes of telemetry will affect many stakeholders such as employees, customers, third party vendors, partners, and others. Therefore, establishing a common goal and purpose across stakeholders helps in creating a compelling argument for telemetry. Our recommendation is to:

- Decide on an executive sponsor who has authority to guide the resources and fund the project (if there is a need)

- Communicate the goal and the purpose to all stakeholders in order to ensure there is a common understanding as to the need for the project and the ultimate results

- Investigate any definitions affecting overall telemetry

- Develop and communicate standards and policies to the stakeholders as well as to cross-functional individuals within the organization

5.1.3 Technology and System Considerations

We live in a fast-changing technological world. Many of the choices we made five years back may not be relevant today, and therefore we must realize that the changes being advocated today may no longer be relevant in a few years. Often, there are two categories of people in an organization: those who are closely associated with a specific technology and religiously follow it no matter what happens around them, and those who are agnostic to any specific technology and are willing to adopt and accept changes in their work environment. For the purpose of gaining traction in your telemetry transformation, we recommend focusing on those in the second category. Such people will be able to focus on the architecture, scalability, and future potential of the proposed change rather than the underlying technology. Individuals in favor of specific technologies will struggle in accepting anything new and will create more challenges. So, spend the time needed to identify those people willing to embrace change and work with them to achieve rapid results.

5.1.4 Impact of Telemetry and Telemetry Data on Existing Business Practices

Telemetry is a public affair in the sense that it demands a high level of accountability, trust, and responsibility within teams handling sensitive data from an outside party. Telemetry's ecosystem is built on mutual respect and trust, and any party who willingly—or even unknowingly—breaks these common norms can become involved in a long legal dispute that could eventually impact the brand and shareholder value. Our advice for all organizations involved is to maintain high standards of ethics and mutual respect for data privacy and protection. We recommend staying away from players or third parties (like service vendors) that lack the experience, discipline, or resources necessary to maintain the highest data protection standards.

5.1.5 Data Protection and Security Obligation

We have emphasized the point of data protection and security in various chapters of this book. Protecting the data and securing it from infiltration is of utmost importance. For this, you must build and maintain the highest levels of data protection practice and security protocols. Then, have some of your most credible and competent technicians deployed to operationalize those protocols.

5.2 DATA OWNERSHIP

A crucial question that often comes up in the process of building a telemetry ecosystem is determining who will be ultimately responsible for the data.
However, there is a clear answer to that question: the data belongs to the end
customer. The purpose of enabling data-driven analytics and edge computing
is to help the end customer gain knowledge and insights on how he or she can
run that business more efficiently. There are organizations that use this data
to enable new business models and create targeted marketing campaigns and
advertisements. Regardless of how the data is used, the owner of the data is
the customer because that is where it was originated, and the customer will
always have complete rights to it.

5.3 TECHNOLOGY OPTIONS FOR TELEMETRY
INFRASTRUCTURE

In Chapters 2 and 4, the telemetry infrastructure elements were introduced with
some of their basic characteristics. In this chapter, we revisit those same elements, this time with a focus on identifying available technology options for
you to consider during implementation. We acknowledge the fast-changing
nature of this domain and technology landscape. So, we urge you to use this
information as a starting point but to always remember to conduct your own
research to ensure you are taking advantage of the latest technology.

In Figure 5.2, we provide an expanded view of the telemetry infrastructure elements, including the collector orchestrator, the initial aggregator,
data lakes, the secondary aggregator, the user interface layer, and API micro
services.

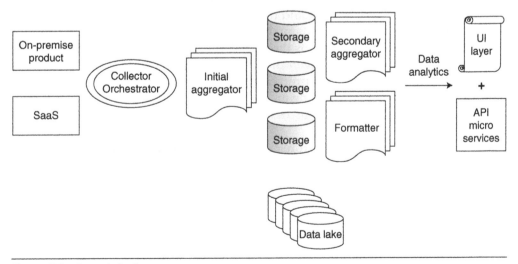

Figure 5.2   Extended telemetry ecosystem.

Moving from left to right in the above figure, there are two types of end products we should consider: one fully and physically within the customer premises and another hosted in the cloud (i.e., SaaS). Depending on the type of end product, the data collection techniques may vary.

The rest of the telemetry ecosystem consists of the following entities:

- The collector orchestrator is the agent that probes and collects the telemetry data. This entity can be either a pull-mode configuration, where it pulls the devices to get the data, or a push-mode configuration, where it waits for the data coming from the end device. In most cases, the collector orchestrator is an industry standard agent.

- The initial aggregator acts as a central hub to bring all the data together from the different end nodes present in the field. The ultimate aim of collecting and correlating the telemetry data is to derive patterns, which requires that data from the different end nodes comes together for analysis.

- Storage can be of various types, depending on the longevity of data usage and speed of processing. It can vary from in-process memory to offline storage. Once collected, data can also be pumped from storage into a data lake for additional correlations and analytics.

- The secondary aggregator is a special-purpose agent that looks for predefined patterns within the primary data sets and moves them to a specific destination for further processing. These aggregators look for explicit instructions, separate the data sets into different streams, and forward it for secondary processing. The process is an intensive and highly involved part of the telemetry ecosystem.

The user interface (UI) layer and the API/micro service layer can be realized in a variety of ways. Though there is no specific standard for this layer, it is vital that the data is represented and insights are in a consumable and consistent format to avoid confusion. Many organizations have started using the insights to make data-driven decisions through the API/micro service level. Carefully orchestrated, workflow-driven processes can make greater use of the telemetry insights to implement procedures and processes to improve the overall product life cycle. Establishing an end-to-end view and building parent–child relationships of data and sources of truth are important to understanding the data flow.

The telemetry infrastructure can be realized through a number of technology options. For the purpose of reviewing these, we use a block diagram consisting of the following elements (see Figure 5.3):

- Data source

- Data ingestion and collection

- Distributed streaming

- Data processing

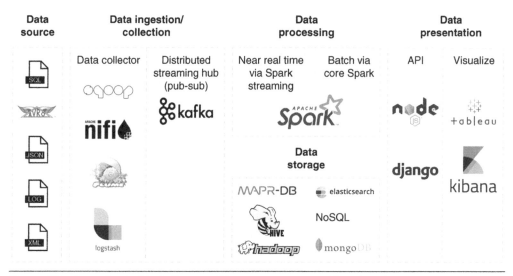

Figure 5.3   Example of a block diagram: Telemetry ecosystem with technical components.

- Data storage

- Data presentation

Each of these blocks represents not only a technology area, but also an organizational or administrative boundary. Therefore, it is important to keep in mind that there can be technical- and process-level handoffs of data involved between these domains. And these domains can exist across multiple organizations or even across multiple countries/geographies.

5.3.1 Data Source

Data sources can be numerous and in diverse formats. The challenge is to ingest data at reasonable speed and process the data efficiently so it can be streamed in real time or ingested in batches. An effective data ingestion process begins by prioritizing data sources, validating individual files, and routing data items to the correct destination. When data is ingested in real time, each data item is imported as it is emitted by the source. When data is ingested in batches, data items are imported in discrete chunks at periodic intervals of time. Before the importing of data begins, it is critical to have a mutual understanding between the customer and your organization on the establishment of a security protocol for the transmission.

5.3.2 Data Ingestion and Collection

Sources of data can be structured or unstructured, real time or bulk. Based on use cases, there are various data collection options. A data collector can be standard or sometimes customized to meet the needs of an organization. The selection of a data collector is often influenced by the type of data, volume of data, frequency of data collection, and transportation of data. It requires deep technical knowledge and should be handled by a qualified technologist with system-level expertise and high awareness of security standards and implementation. While there are various techniques, we will highlight three common methods of data collection available in the market:

- *Apache Sqoop* is used for efficiently transferring bulk data between a structured data store (such as RDBMS) and Hadoop

- *Apache Nifi* helps move data using a flow-based web interface

- *Apache logstash* helps in ingesting and transforming logs, metrics, web application, data stores, and AWS (Amazon Web Service) in a continuous stream

Note that you can customize your data collector solution based on your organizational needs, and the collector can be developed by your internal IT team.

5.3.3 Distributed Streaming

A pipeline to which your applications receive continuous data is known as a "stream." Apache KAFKA is a distributed streaming platform that is horizontally scalable, fault-tolerant, and fast. It simplifies data integration between systems. You need a facility to communicate messages between different system components without these components knowing each other. For this purpose, a pub-sub (publisher-subscriber) event mechanism is used.

There are other technology stacks, like RabbitMQ, that exist in the industry and can be considered for this purpose as well. Most of the telemetry streaming will experience performance degradation and must be designed to consider extreme situations and traffic patterns. In a large-scale network, predicting data patterns and usage is challenging, and deciding the frequency and method of streaming is important and should be accommodated in the design after due consideration of various influencing factors.

5.3.4 Data Processing

Data processing involves systems that are highly scalable and able to perform at a peak level over a period of time. This is an evolving technical area, and many technology stacks are available for your consideration. Attention should be given to big data processing frameworks based on use cases. When it comes to big data, Hadoop provides the MapReduce algorithm, which can split data into smaller processing jobs across the cluster and recombine results in a logical manner. In the Hadoop ecosystem, a Spark processing engine can replace the MapReduce algorithm. This works in-memory and provides faster performance, thus reducing processing time. Note that stream data processing can be achieved by using a streaming data flow engine like Apache Flink as well. Apache Storm is a highly scalable, distributed, real-time computation system used for real-time analytics, and machine learning of high-velocity data.

Again, the technology options that we highlight here are based on our personal experience and knowledge of some of the industry-leading technology stacks. However, this is a highly dynamic area, and several new technical advancements are in-progress when it comes to data processing. There is ongoing research into ways to perform more data processing at the edge device itself and later transport only the processed data to the central cloud. We recommend that you explore the latest trends in the market. More and more network providers are pushing such intelligence to the edge and thereby avoiding huge volumes of traffic and data over a wide-area network.

5.3.5 Data Storage

Emphasis should be given to storing, protecting, and archiving data. A choice is made based on several variables such as security, file system standard, replication, speed, performance, scalability, distribution, and parallel processing (including in-memory abilities). The general trend in the industry has been to move to open-source software based on Hadoop, Spark, Hive, KAFKA, etc. These solutions provide petabyte-scale storage at a fraction of the cost of large-scale databases and provide massive performance leaps over those systems. Data can be accessed for read/write using SQL solutions such as Hive, BEELINE, or DRILL or for NoSQL solutions such as Hbase and MapR-DB using Hadoop Storage.

The following examples illustrate various available technology choices; this list will likely continue to evolve as the application ecosphere evolves:

- *Hadoop.* This technology is a part of Apache Software Foundation. It is a Java-based, open-source programming solution that supports large amounts of data processing and storage in a distributed computing environment. Hadoop stores data in the Hadoop Distributed File System (HDFS). HDFS was designed to handle an append-only format in which, if you have a file in existence, you can add more data to the end of the file. If you want to make any changes earlier in the file, you essentially have to rewrite the entire file with the change in mind. Aggregated data processed on Hadoop can be stored in NoSQL databases, such as Mongo and Cassandra, and custom reports/dashboards can be fed. Outside the Hadoop ecosystem, use cases with requirements of full-text search can be fulfilled by indexing data using elastic search. It is a highly scalable and distributed search engine. APIs are supported.

- *Spark.* To put it simply, we will say that Spark runs on Hadoop. It is an open-source computing framework that allows faster processing and analysis of data.

- *Hive.* This is a tool to process structured data in Hadoop and resides on top of Hadoop to make data queries and analysis easier.

- *KAFKA.* This tool is used for streamlining applications and handling pipelines of real-time data feeds. It is fast and fault tolerant.

- *MapR.* This system distributes Apache Hadoop with its MapR-File System (known as MapR-FS). It provides significantly better performance, reliability, efficiency, maintainability, and ease of use compared to the default HDFS. MapR stores metadata with data in MapR-FS and makes its snapshots consistent. In HDFS, metadata is stored in NameNode and data in DataNode. MapR fully supports random read/write access. If you have a file within your file system, you can access the file at any point, read it, and write to it.

Data storage and archival technologies are also an evolving area. There are vendors who can provide powerful edge-computing solutions that can reduce the need for high-volume centralized data storage. They accomplish this by adding computing and storage power to the edge and then making the node capacity highly scalable. In this case, only processed and relevant data needs to be moved to the central cluster.

5.3.6 Data Presentation

Data presentation is a complex part of the telemetry infrastructure. In most cases, the presentation layer is consumed by engineering users responsible for product development and keen to know how the product is being used in the field. These users are not aware or concerned with the telemetry infrastructure or how the data is collected/formatted. Instead, they want to know what business insights can be extracted (from the data) and how actionable those insights are going to be.

User interface (UI) and user experience (UX) standards are also evolving, and the choices are seemingly unlimited. We are highlighting a few of these options for your consideration:

- *Arcadia* provides powerful data discovery, business intelligence, and visualization in a single integrated platform that runs natively on Hadoop cluster

- *Tableau* provides integration with Hadoop to deliver business insights

- *Kibana* is a visualization plugin for elastic search, making it easier to discover data patterns with time series plotting and to analyze relationships

- You can also build micro services and APIs with Django or Nodejs frameworks

In Figure 5.4 we show an example of an implementation of a scaled-down telemetry ecosystem developed for a specific application.

5.3.7 Data Workflow Considerations

In this section, we focus on the data workflow and how to treat the data at various stages. Keep in mind that the data will take different shapes as it goes

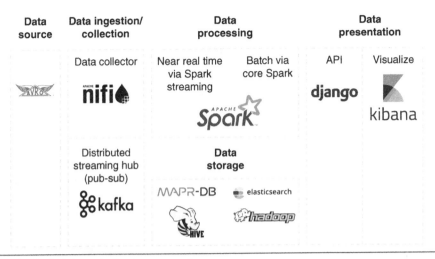

Figure 5.4   Scaled-down technology ecosystem.

through various manipulations and processing before arriving at its final destination. We cannot emphasize enough the criticality of keeping track of the source of truth because doing this enables an audit trail of who does what to the data at each stage.

The end goal of the telemetry infrastructure is to collect, aggregate, and feed product telemetry information to enable cross-functional leaders to analyze and produce meaningful products and business insights. These users then leverage the insights generated to improve customer engagement, improve targeted sales, and enable consistent product subscription renewal:

- A telemetry analytics solution plays a key role in customer success as it consumes, stores, and provides analytics on all telemetry data collected

- Telemetry data in Apache AVRO (serialized data) can be posted to a public cloud service provider on a simple storage service (S3) bucket by the collector

There are many systems or tools available for data storage, data search, data serialization, and related activities. To illustrate, here are some examples:

- *Producer Spark Job* will be "listening" to Amazon Simple Queue Service (SQS) when an AVRO file is posted on an S3 bucket and an SQS message is sent out. This will trigger the producer job to download the file. It will infer the schema and transform the data into serialized AVRO records and post the records into KAFKA Topic for that particular device type.

- *Consumer Spark Streaming Job* consumes the batch of records from respective topics and persists into the telemetry data store in the big data platform MapR-DB.

- *Scheduled Hive to Elastic Search Spark Job* indexes data for quick search. API with the Django framework and visualization using Kibana helps to discover and represent the telemetry data. Django is a high-level Python web framework that allows experienced developers to do rapid developments. Kibana is a visualization layer.

Figure 5.5 is a data flow diagram that gives you a basic understanding on how this technology is built and deployed. Note that there are other techniques to address the data flows, but we will not venture too deeply into those technologies.

Architecture is evolving with use cases in each new release. It started with a fixed schema for data ingestion. However, now we can use a schema-less write architecture, which provides high writing throughput and faster onboarding of new products for telemetry. Telemetry system design is highly dependent on the use cases and how the data is going to be consumed by the end user. It also depends on the type of end device and the volume of data to be processed and transported. You should always have a provision for horizontal and vertical expansion of the architecture to make sure the entire system is scalable and replicable for current use and also for the future.

The data ingestion diagram in Figure 5.5 demonstrates an end-to-end flow to help you visualize the big picture. Note that the data store is tuned to faster write and read based on use cases. MapR-DB (Hbase) supports faster writes, and Hive supports faster reads. MapR-DB through columnar families gives greater control for schema-less data on writes and reduces maintenance with high throughput for writes.

Ingestion of telemetry data through the producer/consumer has been evolving over time. Development efforts are centered on minimizing code changes required to ingest telemetry data when new devices (products) are onboarded or when existing device (product) attributes are altered during the release cycle of the product. A data catalog was introduced to maintain schema information across products. With any changes to an AVRO schema, the on-demand catalog update job is executed, which ensures the schemas are updated across products.

Using advanced features of Spark—such as dynamic building of data frames and columnar store in MapR-DB, along with cataloging and mapping the problem statement of onboarding different products with different telemetry attributes—was addressed. The end state is to make this process fully automated and capable of handling telemetry data across products and customers using different patches at any given time.

Spark Elastic search Sync Job syncs the data from telemetry and the historic data store to elastic search. APIs are built with the Python-based Django framework to expose telemetry data. Also, Kibana dashboards are available for visualizing telemetry data.

All the custom jobs are coded in Scala/Java using an Apache Spark Directed Acyclic Graph (DAG) Processing Engine. The external Hive View is exposed to downstream applications, which will merge telemetry data with other master/transaction data to provide business insights around customer success use cases.

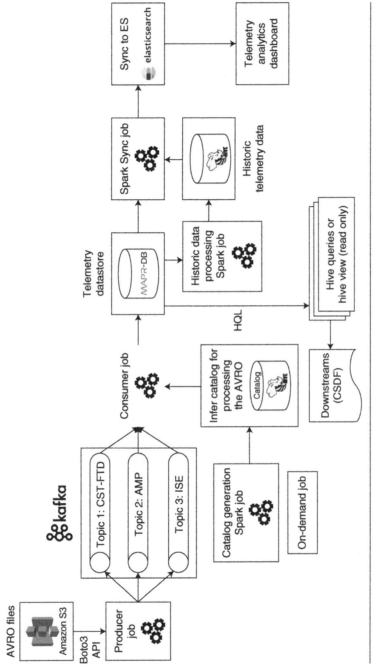

Figure 5.5 Data ingestion technology.

5.4 ONBOARDING OF THE CUSTOMERS

Customer onboarding needs to be handled carefully and requires a great deal of planning. We discuss a few options and identify possible obstacles that you may encounter in your telemetry journey.

Let's consider a few facts before onboarding a customer:

- Telemetry data, by virtue of being associated with the customer, has customer-specific and confidential data embedded. There are specific laws that affect how this data is stored, accessed, and distributed.

- There are country-specific laws that impose restrictions on who can access the data, where this data can reside, who is going to use the data, what purpose the data is used for, and also what disclosures need to be made.

- The destination company needs to inform the customer how this data will be used and by whom. Also, there must be strong data protection standards agreed upon and established before data collection begins.

- The company receiving the data must standardize collectors and data formats to ease universal acceptance across the company. Standardization will reduce the complexity of instrumentation and troubleshooting. Having standards across the organization will allow sales, marketing, support, and engineering to define a high-level picture for communicating and obtaining agreement from various stakeholders.

5.5 POLICY AND GOVERNANCE

The most important outcome when implementing policy and governance for telemetry is to give employees clear guidance and confidence in the leadership and management teams. Governance leads to better consistency of processes and provides in-depth insights. Before telemetry becomes the main part of your customer listening program, you need to ensure certain things are in place:

- *Taxonomy.* First and foremost for any organization planning to collect telemetry data is to define a common taxonomy across the company. This taxonomy includes the naming conventions, formats, and agreements. Having a common and universal taxonomy will help both decision makers and engineers make decisions based on the data and talk the same language. A companywide committee or council needs to be set up to define the standards and taxonomy, and documents must be version controlled.

- *Interface format.* An agreement must be reached among all players on how the external facing interface will be defined. Having standard interfaces will avoid duplication of work efforts and lessen confusion for customers who may use different types of products from the same company.

- *Use cases.* Insights from telemetry data will eventually force policy makers to change the business course and agree to collective measures for improving the product's prospects in the market. It is important to have appropriate use cases defined at a product level and agreed to by all parties in the decision chain. In many situations, engineering and support teams starts collecting data without having a proper use case in mind and later struggle to handle the huge influx of data. Our advice is to define use cases first and only collect the data needed to serve those use cases. Having a use case–driven data collection approach allows you to be precise and data collection to be efficient.

- *Security standards.* Having a security framework and a strong security standard is of the utmost importance. Both you and your customer should know what security standards are in place and must collaborate on implementing them. Security is like a switch—either you are fully secured or you are not secured at all. So, it is important to establish the norms, taxonomy, procedure, and standards of security before even thinking of onboarding a customer.

- *Frequency.* How often data is accessed and collected may sound like a moot point. Remember, we are dealing with a huge volume of data as well as transporting the data over the network to a different location. We also need to discuss storing and processing the data. Consider the analogy of repairing a road during peak traffic hours versus early morning hours when the traffic is at a minimum. The impact during peak hours is huge, and drivers will have a totally negative driving experience. Telemetry data collection should take into account traffic patterns and usage patterns of the network so as to not result in a negative experience for your customers. The provider and receiver of data need to agree on the timings and associated standards.

- *Data ownership.* Ownership of data and usage of data needs to be agreed upon by all parties involved. This is one area that should be under contractual agreement so that both parties are legally protected. This will help avoid any future litigation related to data sharing.

- *Data protection.* Data protection standards need to be defined and clearly communicated to all parties in the ecosystem. Everyone must know what standards are used and how often those standards are reviewed and updated.

- *Storage and archival.* If the data is stored for future usage, it should be agreed to by all parties in the ecosystem. Data archival policies should be well established and published to all stakeholders.

5.6 TELEMETRY ECOSYSTEM STAKEHOLDERS

Collecting data from a customer involves a number of players. While an outside observer could conclude that this is a matter of moving data from one place to another over a network, it is more complex and involves more legal bindings than imagined. Figure 5.6 provides a simplified illustration of the

Figure 5.6 Telemetry personas.

various organizations and personas involved with a large-scale telemetry defined network. While these are typical roles, we believe they represent the minimal set of personas required.

To begin with, customers are never willing to give proprietary data away unless there is a clear incentive or value for them to do so. The decision on what the incentive is depends on the level of influence and circumstances involved. The executive leadership does not play a role in handling data and the related technology; however, they are crucial when it comes to decision making. Similarly, each of these personas plays a unique role in the entire telemetry project. Our experience shows that a successful telemetry implementation needs active support all the way to the CEO and his or her staff, including the chief financial officer, the head of sales, etc. In fact, these people will be involved in approving financial incentives or discounts necessary to entice the customer to share the data. It is also important to have channel and sales partners involved in order to influence customers—at the time of sale—to include the telemetry rights and articulate an attractive return on investment for sharing the data. The incentive can be as trivial as offering to freely share the analytics and insights from the collected data. This approach can help create upgrade opportunities in the customer network and/or provide sales discount for a replacement product. The most important thing here is to engage customers early enough in the sales cycle to get a legal agreement for sharing telemetry data.

Here is a comprehensive list of the different personas involved and a brief description of their respective roles:

- *Executive leadership.* This set includes chief executive officer (CEO), chief financial officer (CFO), and general manager (GM) of a product unit. Also included are leaders of key functional areas such as sales and manufacturing. These players oversee the success of the project and remove any roadblocks.

- *Services and support.* This organization is responsible for collecting data because it has access to the customer network as part of the troubleshooting process and/or it was likely involved in the design of the customer network. Service and support engineers have the necessary experience to handle large volumes of data in the form of logs and kernel dumps.

- *Legal and brand protection.* This group needs to be consulted and informed to make sure the company is protected from a legal standpoint in case of a dispute.

- *Finance.* This department generally decides on the financial aspects of the relationship and transactions.

- *IT.* The chief information officer (CIO) and the IT department build the backbone of the data exchange and all relevant activities of storage, process, protection, and destruction of the data.

- *Sales and marketing.* The direct and indirect sales channels are involved to influence the customer to share the data.

- *Customer.* The most important and largest stakeholder is the customer whose data is being collected.

- *Engineering.* Engineers are the ones who originally created the product and consume the telemetry feedback about the product.

5.7 TELEMETRY LEGAL FRAMEWORK AND POTENTIAL RISKS

Let us now consider some common aspects of the telemetry ecosystem and how legal and compliance issues play a much bigger role than in any normal software or manufacturing process. By virtue of being the act of collecting and transporting data from one entity to another, this process is fraught with complexity in terms of policies and procedures. Here are some key considerations as you work toward building a telemetry infrastructure:

- Telemetry drawbacks
- Telemetry risk factors

We now examine each of these topics in more detail.

5.7.1 Telemetry Drawbacks

So far, we have focused on the positive aspects of telemetry and how impactful the entire infrastructure can be when properly implemented. However, like everything else in life, there are challenges or drawbacks that come with it, and you must be fully aware of them as you engage in a telemetry program. Here are some of the primary ones:

- It requires handling and protection of very large volumes of data

- It requires a permanent and significant investment in infrastructure and people

- The inability to convert the telemetry data into insights and, ultimately, into action across the organization can turn your telemetry program into a wasted investment

- The "shelf life" of data in storage must be decided upfront; otherwise, the cost of storage and upkeep of data can quickly escalate

5.7.2 Telemetry Risk Factors

There are a number of risk factors that should be considered before embarking on the telemetry journey (see Table 5.1).

Table 5.1 Telemetry risk factors.

Consideration	Risk factor
Country-specific compliance	Certain countries and regions have laws that limit what/how data can be taken out of the country. Data center and other key elements of telemetry infrastructure must be located in the same jurisdiction for processing the data.
Responsibility and accountability	The ownership and accountability of data must be documented. This can have legal consequences if not managed carefully.
Probes and connectors	Where (in the data path) the probes and connectors are inserted (to collect the data) needs to be disclosed. Hidden probes or connectors can easily carry legal, financial, and brand consequences for the organization.
Security compliance	Data protection standards like those in the EU (and similar ones in the United States and other countries) need to be followed. This requires training your personnel and maintaining their level of competency.
Data destruction	Destruction of data needs to be recorded. Records need to be maintained to enable future audits.
Standards and norms	Industry standards around data exchange protocols and data mining techniques can sometimes be in conflict with private standards. Agreeing on common standards of data exchange can sometimes be a challenge.
Financial	Legal and financial compliance can become a huge issue. Because data is usually collected from various countries or jurisdictions, it adds more complexity in drafting companywide policy agreements.
Personally identifiable information (PII)	There is always a significant risk associated with handling and holding PII data of a third party. Any leakage of such data can carry legal, financial, and brand consequences for the organization.

5.8 BRINGING IT ALL TOGETHER: THE ART AND SCIENCE OF TELEMETRY DESIGN

In this chapter, we have examined various technical aspects of an organization preparing to adopt a telemetry program. Research and industry data indicate that by 2020, more than 50 billion end points will be digitally connected to the internet. Every factory floor and every manufacturing industry will have one or more digital end points. The Internet of Things (IoT) and digitally designed manufacturing will no longer be abstract concepts but will become the norm across the global economy. The rate at which the industry is changing, in terms of connected devices, is unprecedented. The growth in the number of connected devices, even when normalized by the human population, is expected to grow exponentially from 2014 to 2020.[1] Each of these devices will be in a position to send telemetry data. Those who believe that IoT is nothing more than a connected fridge or camera are in for a big surprise.

To illustrate the criticality and urgency of data collection through telemetry, we will use a seemingly remote use case. While we admit this case sounds somewhat futuristic today, we expect it will become the norm in the near future.

Let us consider a farmer in a remote village in India who has no access to any modern technology, much less access to the internet. In a country like India, with a growing population and unpredictable rain patterns, it is alarmingly risky for a farmer to invest the money in agriculture without aid from the government. How can the government make a difference in the farmer's decision making? In India today, we find that most of the farming is unorganized, with the majority of the farmland owned by farmers with less than a hectare of land. Now the question is, Can the same telemetry principles and technology mentioned in the previous chapters be put to use for the village farmer?

Fortunately, the answer to the question is yes. In fact, it is already being tried in various locales. All it takes is to deploy tiny sensors in the field and connect them with an aggregator for data consolidation. The nature of these sensors can vary widely, ranging from things like soil quality indicators to wetness indicators to fertilizer analyzers. The data can then be analyzed, and appropriate decisions can be made such as whether it is viable to continue to invest in the farm.

Now, let us consider the case of a heavily organized farm of the type seen with ranch owners in the United States. The same principles of telemetry can be applied with little or no modification of the fundamentals. We can have centralized data management that is inclusive of data elements ranging from the soil all way to the supermarket shelf. Data analysis could suggest to the ranch owner the best time to take the product to market and which supermarket chain can offer the best price. Alternatively, the same data analysis on the other side of the spectrum can help the supermarket chain to determine which side of the country has ranchers ready with product supply.

The only limit here is our ability to imagine possible use cases, realizing such cases with data and data science will become more prominent in the next 10 years.

To summarize, the first step in telemetry is defining the purpose and making sure the decision makers believe in the end goal of implementing processes based on telemetry data to improve customer relations and creating a positive customer experience. Once the big picture is established, the next step is to find the change agents and define the standards or engagements with the telemetry project. With the decision makers, change agents, and purpose in hand, you will be able to drive a companywide cultural change that incorporates telemetry-based organizational principles and practices.

If you are a decision maker within a company, such as a CEO or CIO, who has not given a thought to the concepts of telemetry, then it is time to change. Data gathering can be accomplished through satellite links, and end-user interfaces can be kiosks in the local administrative office of a village. The possibilities are unlimited for those with imagination and willingness to embrace telemetry with all its opportunities and challenges.

Telemetry and digitization are not two different paradigms. They are complementary and need each other to make the leapfrog disruption happen. What you digitize needs to be measured, and how you measure the digitization is through data collection via telemetry. The age-old theory says that what gets measured gets improved. What gets improved creates opportunities for more digitization.

Whether you are dealing with humans or machines, feedback is the most essential factor in improving the learning and making it better for tomorrow and for the next generation. Being practitioners of telemetry-based design will allow you to ride the next wave of the internet evolution and revolution! If you have not started, we encourage you to swim fast so that this wave does not leave you behind.

NOTE

1. Gil Press, "9 new predictions and market assessments for the Internet of Things (IoT)," *Forbes.com*, July 30, 2015, retrieved November 11, 2017.

6

Conclusions

In this chapter, we summarize the salient points of the book and discuss concepts like digitization, quality, and telemetry that are impacting/disrupting companies across the world economy. For digitization, we outline the basic elements of this transformation, including an introduction of the digital framework. We then use a case study to illustrate how digitization can be applied to quality. Then, we discuss critical-to-quality processes and what would be required to digitize them. We next explore the impact that telemetry data is already having through a set of popular applications. Finally, we close with a checklist that can help organizations to better engage in the business of creating, consuming, or processing data telemetry.

This chapter is organized into the following sections:

1. Quality experience telemetry review

2. Digital transformation quest

3. Digitization of quality

4. Telemetry data in action: current applications

5. Telemetry project checklist

6.1 QUALITY EXPERIENCE TELEMETRY REVIEW

We have dedicated this book to the study of telemetry data and its potential use to drive continuous improvements in customer experience. The real-time nature of the data and the advent of machine-learning algorithms have set the stage for a new era we call *adaptive customer experience*. These capabilities are creating an unprecedented opportunity to change the relationship between customers and the systems they depend on in their digital world.

Telemetry itself can be considered a by-product of today's technology trends like digitization and Internet of Things (IoT). So, it is important to understand the concepts behind these trends as they affect the global economy. They are driving changes in customer expectations, value delivery, and business modes across industries.

Leveraging telemetry requires a solid foundation on data. It is important to start this journey with a good understanding of basic data structures, organizational approaches, database types, and big data. It is also important to understand the basic concepts behind data quality and data security. Companies are making large capital investments in building the infrastructure required to support telemetry. It is important to understand the basic elements of that infrastructure and how to best interact with it to extract data.

From a people perspective, data scientists are the key players in the telemetry field. They have the necessary mastery of underlying data principles needed to implement telemetry programs. They not only help create the necessary infrastructure to collect, house, and manage telemetry data, but also drive efforts to turn data into actionable insights.

Given our stated focus of using telemetry data to drive customer experience improvement, we see the need to have a strong foundation of quality and quality management principles. These principles include, but are not limited to, the definition of metrics, customer listening, and root cause analysis. The establishment of quality governance forums is a best practice to ensure that insights turn into actions. Change management and approaches to create sustainability of improvements are also foundational.

In this book, we use "customer success" as an example of a business model that is highly dependent on telemetry data. This model is being widely adopted by software as a service (SaaS) companies. The idea behind this model is to get the sales force to think about a broader customer life cycle that includes adopt, expand, and renew, in addition to the traditional sale. Customer success and customer experience are highly intertwined, so it is important to understand the differences and similarities.

Finally, we need to get into applications that bring telemetry to life for the business. In our increasingly digitized world, the proliferation of sensors and improvements in data science capabilities create an environment where possibilities (for telemetry) are limitless. Imagination is the only ingredient that needs to be added to turn telemetry data into valuable insights for people and businesses across the global economy.

6.2 DIGITAL TRANSFORMATION QUEST

Today, many companies are embracing digitization as a way to remain competitive in a business environment that requires a lower cost of operation, higher speed, and simplicity. In addition to simply changing the format of information from paper to digital, these transformations are anchored around a greater dependency on software application, data centers, and cloud technologies. Honestly, this can feel like a hugely ambitious and daunting task. It requires a transformation of every aspect of how the company works from sales to engineering to marketing to supply chain to support. And, like the proverbial "change the engines on the plane while in mid-flight," companies must do this while continuing to meet shareholder return expectations.

Generally speaking, digital transformation involves three key steps:

1. Creating a baseline

2. Assessing gap to target

3. Implementation

6.2.1 Creating a Baseline

The digitization journey always starts with establishing a baseline (or basic understanding) of current capability. These assessments are done at the corporate level as well as within each impacted function. They are grouped into three main buckets:

1. *Process.* This assessment focuses on an inventory of the company's existing operational processes, especially the ones most critical to the business. It includes, but is not limited to:
   — Development processes
   — Sales processes
   — Quality and compliance
   — Marketing processes
   — Technical support processes
   — Human resource processes
   — Legal and government affairs processes

2. *People.* This assessment targets employee capability. Like the process assessment, it starts with an inventory of current capability. These capabilities include education, experience, job performance, and skills. In addition, a site strategy component is added to understand where the existing workforce is deployed geographically and whether they are remote or co-located with major corporate centers.

3. *Technology.* This assessment focuses on computer systems and tools. Again, this involves an inventory of existing capability. It is typically managed by the information technology (IT) of the company. However, function-specific systems are also included.

6.2.2 Gap Assessment

Once the baseline is complete, we are ready to assess the gap to target. But for that, we need to answer the question, What is the target? The target (or end state) is where the company wants to be once the transformation is complete. The end state is usually defined by the senior most leaders of the company, and it has two primary components:

1. Vision

2. Strategy

Vision is delivered in the form of statement that seeks to answer the *what* (i.e., what are we trying to accomplish with this effort; what is success; what does it look like?). The time horizon of the vision statement is generally five years, and it should include enough information to captivate the ambition, imagination, and energy of its intended audience. A perfect example of a great vision statement is the one delivered by former president of the United States John F. Kennedy in a speech to Congress on May 25, 1961. At the time, the United States was feeling demoralized by a string of failures as the nation attempted to match the space technology of the Soviet Union. The efforts driven by the newly created National Aeronautics and Space Administration (NASA) appeared to lack focus. During his speech, the president said: "I believe that this nation should commit itself to achieving the goal, before this decade is out, of landing a man on the moon and returning him safely to the Earth."[1] That goal represented the perfect combination of ambition and challenge. It served as a galvanizing force across NASA, the federal government, and the nation as a whole. The nation beamed with pride when the goal was realized with the moon landing orchestrated by NASA in July 1969.

Strategy is subordinate to the vision, and it seeks to answer the *how* (i.e., how are we going to achieve our vision?). The time horizon of the strategy statements tends to be three years. The strategy statement is typically comprised of multiple sub-statements, each speaking to an element of the strategy. Another way of looking at these elements is to consider them "levers" that you will "push" in order to accomplish the vision. A best practice is to keep the number of elements in a strategy statement to no more than three to ensure they are memorable (i.e., can be easily remembered). Specific to digital transformations, leading companies invariably include as one of their strategic elements the definition, socialization, and adoption of a common framework. This digital framework serves as a map to help members of the company understand the steps required in getting to the target. While it varies slightly from company to company, the digital framework typically involves the following five steps:

1. Streamline

2. Automate

3. Protect

4. Observe

5. Upgrade

Figure 6.1 depicts the cycle associated with the digital framework. Normally, companies undertaking a digital transformation would start at the top with "streamline" and then move clockwise in this cycle. That does not preclude organizations from starting at any other step (say, automation) if a digital capability is already in place and this framework is being applied to enhance it.

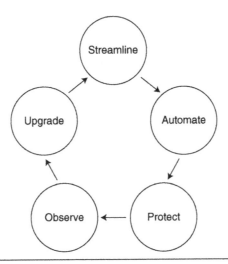

Figure 6.1 Digital framework.

6.2.2.1 *Streamline*

Streamlining involves taking existing processes and simplifying them as much as possible. Typically, existing processes evolve over time and tend to get increasingly complex. Also, elements of the process become obsolete and need to be deprecated.

6.2.2.2 *Automate*

Once the process has been simplified, it is ready for automation. Like any software development activity, automation of the existing process occurs incrementally. Everything starts with a minimum viable product (MVP) that is defined to include a subset of the capabilities in the process but sufficient to make it valuable to users. In addition to software development, this step is heavy on change management, which orchestrates the definition of the MVP and subsequent user stories. Additionally, it works with stakeholders to drive adoption of automated processes.

6.2.2.3 *Protect*

As processes are digitized, an important priority is minimizing exposure to malicious cyberattacks from inside or outside the company. As discussed in Chapter 3 in the context of data security, these efforts can be grouped into the following action areas (Table 6.1):

- Design
- Monitoring
- Response
- Remediation

Table 6.1 Digital protection actions.

Action	Description
Design	The data infrastructure (network, servers, databases) is designed to be resilient to cyberattack. Networks are designed with multilayer defense in mind. This ensures that even if one portion of the network is compromised, access to the rest of the network is not guaranteed. Finally, use of data encryption is widespread as a final line of defense to prevent unauthorized use of information.
Monitoring	Operation centers are staffed around the clock to oversee traffic and data consumption patterns. Detection capabilities are continuously enhanced to keep pace with the ever-improving intrusion capabilities of cyber criminals. Once a detection is verified, information is shared with the response team to activate countermeasures.
Response	Working closely with the monitoring resources, this area focuses on defining and implementing a playbook of responses to cyberattacks. A typical response involves isolating the portion of the network that has been compromised. Sometimes, active responses can be undertaken where the specific source of the attack is identified. These responses could include disrupting traffic flow from the offending source or informing law enforcement authorities.
Remediation	Once an attack has been isolated or neutralized, efforts are made to restore the information to its pre-attack state; if that is not possible, the information is deleted. Then an investigation is carried out to identify lessons learned and recommend actions that would prevent and/or minimize similar attacks in the future. These lessons learned are typically translated into enhanced policies and procedures.

6.2.2.4 *Observe*

Process effectiveness needs to be constantly monitored to ensure desired outcomes are being achieved. Monitoring is typically achieved using metrics. In-process metrics are defined and trends are visualized in dashboards. In-process metrics tend to fall into three primary categories:

1. *Adoption.* These metrics track the consumption of the process across its intended population. Adoption metrics are typically used by management to drive calls to action and ensure people are following through on their commitments to use these processes.

2. *Effectiveness.* These metrics assess the level to which the processes are delivering their intended outcomes. You may have created a highly automated process that operates securely, but if it does not fully achieve its basic intent, its effectiveness is low.

3. *Efficiency.* These metrics tend to track cycle time associated with the process. This tends to be associated with operational rigor—for example, mean time between failures.

6.2.2.5 *Upgrade*

Based on the observations in the previous step, enhancements are continuously made to the process to ensure it remains effective. Additionally, the upgrade step looks for input outside of the existing process (e.g., from industry or academia) to ensure existing processes are not becoming obsolete due to technology or market transitions.

6.2.3 Implementation

Vision and strategy statements can only go so far; at some point, you need people to actually execute a project plan that moves them through the digital framework. At the corporate level, there is typically an officer-level leader—a chief digitization officer (CDO)—who has responsibility for moving the overall transformation forward. That leader would have a cross-functional team of managers who help drive corporate efforts but, more importantly, ensure that function-specific execution is aligned with the digital transformation plan. These cross-functional members push for clarity of what their functions are expected to do, but also what other functions expect from them (i.e., interdependencies). Successful organizations create multilevel governance to ensure clarity of decision making across large enterprises. There are two basic levels:

1. *Corporate.* At the corporate level, decisions and operational tracking of the digital transformation actions will be at a higher level of abstraction. However, the information needs to be granular enough to ascertain status and the accountability clear enough to assign ownership for action. Once again, metrics are used to monitor progress. The company-level abstractions of the metrics get reviewed at the corporate board level, usually chaired by the CDO.

2. *Functional.* At the function level, decision and operational tracking will be at a level commensurate with the functional contribution to the transformational effort. As with the corporate governance board, functional boards need the active engagement and sponsorship of functional leaders. The CDO plays a key role in ensuring function-specific sponsors are identified and these individuals are engaged. *There is no substitute for this!* In the absence of leadership engagement, boards become dysfunctional.

Beyond leadership and common metrics, operational rigor is the next required ingredient for success. When metrics do not meet the preestablished goals, actions need to be assigned by the leaders with clear expectations of resolution time. A discipline of reviewing and tracking the status of assigned actions until resolution should be emphasized.

Summarizing, companies undergoing digital transformations tend to follow a relatively similar three-step process: creating a baseline, assessing gap to target, and implementation. However, the complexity of the change varies greatly depending on where the company starts (baseline), the size of the company, and how ambitious its target state is. The following case study helps better illustrate the forces behind digitization and the challenges associated with this undertaking.

Case Study: Digitizing SRJ Corporation

To illustrate, let's define a fictional technology company called Systems Really Jazzy (SRJ for short). SRJ has a track record of success in the consumer products business, but revenue growth has stagnated in recent years, leading to stagnation in the stock price as well. In the good old days, SRJ would deliver products to its customers, and the moment the merchandise hit the customer's premises, SRJ would receive full payment. It was then up to the customer to monetize the investment by putting those assets into production. Sometimes these products would not work as expected, and customers had to work with SRJ for hardware and/or software fixes, which in turn led to further delays on monetizing the customer's investment. For SRJ, these were the golden days because it received full payment for its delivered inventory regardless of whether the customer was able to put the inventory into production or not. Bottom line, customers absorbed all the risk associated with the investment.

However, new technologies have emerged that challenge SRJ's market dominance. These technologies rely on software built on top of commoditized hardware to deliver products of equivalent value to SRJ's product portfolio. The use of software not only opens the door for faster development cycles, but also significantly changes the cost side of the equation. Therefore, companies developing products based on this new technology could offer products of equivalent value, but at a significantly lower price point. To make things even worse for SRJ, these new competitors deliver value in the form of software subscription. SRJ has zero experience in software subscription and recurring revenue business. So, even if it wants to respond in kind to these competitors, SRJ lacks the capability to do so. When confronted with this new modality, many customers are choosing to try the new companies' offerings. After trying, they discover they really like the aspect of software subscription that allows them—for the first time—to share the investment risk with their providers. The barrier for adoption of alternative providers is suddenly lower than it has ever been. In the final analysis, these developments are leading to an erosion of SRJ's market position relative to competitors.

Taking advantage of their newly found leverage, SRJ's traditional customers are pressuring SRJ to lower its cost and deliver value as a software service. SRJ has to somehow meet this challenge if it wants to retain business or face continuous erosion in its market share.

Faced with this threat, the CEO of SRJ commits to a digital transformation process to respond to market dynamics and reposition the company for success. The CEO defines a vision that moves the company over a period of three years from product centricity to software as a service (subscription and recurring revenue). Additionally, the CEO names a CDO from his staff, and she begins defining the strategy and execution plans. The CDO launches a series of companywide communications intended to educate the whole company on the vision, strategy, and the digital transformation framework. Additionally, the CDO launches a cross-functional steering committee that would help drive execution at the corporate and functional levels.

As time moved on, tension mounted within the company as customers kept moving away from the existing product-based offers at a faster rate than adoption of the new software subscription services. Nevertheless, the CDO remained calm and kept the organization focused on developing new, recurring revenue offers. She was successful in enrolling the employee base into the transformation by hosting town hall–type meetings where not only updates were provided, but suggestions were sought and listened to.

Despite the market tendency to react negatively to unpredictability, analyst consensus was to give SRJ's CEO time to implement the transformation plan as long as evidence of progress continued to be shown. Within 36 months of the start of the transformation, the company was able to introduce software subscription offers in every element of its portfolio, including core markets. This allowed SRJ to fend off market pressures and start offering competitive SRJ-based solutions that prevented further erosion in market share.

In terms of software subscription operations, SRJ embraced a huge change in the way it sold and supported customers. It shifted to using the customer success model[2] as the basis for its new sales operations. This model teaches sales employees that closing the sale is only the beginning of a journey that includes getting customers to adopt what they bought and removing any barriers in their realization of value. If they are successful in removing adoption barriers, then subscription renewals will be a nonissue and likely lead to expanded sales. This new approach resonated with customers who always felt SRJ was not sharing the investment risk with them.

While SRJ continued the process of digitizing all of its internal processes beyond the three-year mark, the ability to quickly deliver competitive SaaS offers and the adoption of a customer success model allowed the company to stabilize market share. While only time can tell if SRJ will dominate the market the same way it did before, the quick action by the CEO undoubtedly enabled the company to turn the tide with its customers and put it back on a path of success.

6.3 DIGITIZATION OF QUALITY

In Chapter 3, we discussed the concept of adaptive customer experience through telemetry data. The premise of that concept is that real-time availability of customer experience data opens the door for real-time responses based on pre-deployed machine-learning algorithms. However, besides the real-time responses, there is still a need for some of the data to be sent and shared with the software provider for more systemic improvements. This section speaks to that scenario and how the company's internal processes need to be adapted to consume such information.

For starters, let's refresh your memory as to where customer experience data comes from today. In Chapter 3, Section 3.6, we explained that most of the data used to measure customer experience currently come from analysis of customer calls. Customer call data (volume, resolution code, product association) is typically processed once a month, at which point, downstream metrics based on the data are updated. Depending on the metric, a statistically significant change in trends will not raise an alert until it happens for at least two reporting cycles (two months) in a row. At this point, there is at least a two-month lag from the moment of the customer's negative experience that triggered the call.

Additionally, as we explained, due to metric normalization (e.g., install base) applied to remove noise, a small (relative to total population) number of issues will not cause the metric to move outside of its control range. Analogous to turning a large ship versus a small boat, strategic metrics won't move unless a significant portion of the install base experience a problem. So again, this set of customer calls will not trigger a systemic corrective action until the problem becomes more pervasive.

Companies tend to tailor their business operations around quarterly business reviews (QBRs). These forums occur at different levels within the company, and they are designed to prepare and review the information needed to create financial reports for investors. Customer experience and quality data is typically reviewed in QBR forums, and the monthly/quarterly cycle time of data updating fits nicely into that business cadence.

With the advent of real-time customer experience data, there is an opportunity to consume the information differently and accelerate time to action. A path to achieve that builds on the concept of digitization we discussed in the previous section, but it specifically focuses on operational processes targeting quality. We call those processes critical-to-quality processes.

6.3.1 Digitizing Critical-to-Quality Processes

The concept of *critical-to-quality (CTQ)* processes is not new. CTQ is part of the total quality management methodology[3] and is also a principle enshrined in Six Sigma[4] training. CTQ processes are a subset of the company's operational processes that play a central role in the quality that customer's experience. For example, the software release management process is considered critical to quality because it helps define the acceptable quality before making software available to customers.

As we discussed in the previous section, digital transformations entail digitizing the company's operational processes. If we target those that are critical to quality first, we enable the company to consume/respond to changes in the customer experience faster than ever. Identifying what is critical to quality is not hard because most of those processes are well known and managed. The bigger challenge is to get the cross-functional commitment to move these processes through the digital framework. Two examples of the critical-to-quality process being digitized by leading companies follow.

6.3.1.1 Digitizing Customer Listening

Capturing the voice of customer is one of those critical-to-quality processes in any company. It essentially entails eliciting, capturing, analyzing, and socializing the voice of customer regardless of the modality in which it is captured. There are different ways to "hear" the voice of customer, including analyzing customer calls (as we just discussed) as well as running customer survey programs like customer satisfaction (CSAT) or Net Promoter Score™ (NPS). Unlike customer calls, which reflect direct customer pain, customer surveys capture customers' sentiments about their interaction with the company. Generally speaking, customer feedback falls into two groups:

1. *Experiential.* This feedback comes as a result of specific interactions between the customer and company's products or services. It is typically captured through customer calls, hardware returns, and now through quality telemetry. This data is considered highly actionable because you can trace things to a particular failure and can troubleshoot it in the system. However, experiential feedback also tends to be very transactional, so it is hard to get an overall picture of the customer's journey from a series of discrete failures. For example, software defects encountered by customers are classified as experiential data.

2. *Emotional.* This feedback reflects the customer's perception about the company. Depending on the customer role, that perception might be shaped through a series of direct experiences or indirectly through peers. Actionability is a traditional challenge with emotional data. The customer is angry, but it might be hard to figure out exactly why. Verbatim or free-text input is typically captured to help with the actionability challenge, but it is not as effective as experiential data. On the other hand, perception is typically associated with a history of interactions as opposed to just one (a sum of experiences). So, perception tends to provide a truer reflection of customer sentiment. Customer surveys are the primary vehicles to capture customer perception.

A best practice is to have the voice of customer process centralized. However, many companies don't do this, and as a result there are many internal functions concurrently playing in this space. Imagine engineering teams collecting the voice of customer for their products, while the technical support center collects the same for its services (just to name two functions)—and all of these requests for feedback come to customers in a highly uncoordinated fashion. To make matters worse, the information is internally kept in functional silos and not shared. This lack of coordination creates an increasingly frustrating situation for customers because they are asked to provide the same feedback repeatedly by multiple sides of the company. To make matters worse, some companies lack a common customer identifier convention, so multiple functions are collecting feedback from the same customer but recording it using different customer identifiers, so even if they want to share data, they can't!

Leading companies have the ability to collect intelligence from social media feeds. While social media data can usually be categorized as emotional data, its very nature allows users to post information that could be considered experiential as well. There are examples of social media data that is used as an early warning indicator for customer escalations. In that application, it has been proven to be predictive of customer calls to the technical assistance center.

If you are looking to digitize the customer listening process, you must figure a way to integrate customer data that currently exist across silos. You will need both experiential sources as well as emotional sources. A data science capability known as *data threading* is key to enabling integration of data across silos. The ability to say "This is what customer X is telling us" across multiple experiential and emotional channels is a good first step.

Once we have successfully threaded existing data, we are in a position to bring telemetry (real-time) data into the mix. We could then envision a fully automated processes that allow internal stakeholders to consume voice-of-customer data as a service, including application program interfaces (APIs).

We could then imagine an internal stakeholder like engineering—for example, building an algorithm that queries the voice-of-customer database as it gets ready to validate software readiness to ship. The algorithm could be checking the latest feedback on previous versions of this software as well as early deployments of the current version. The algorithm could then request additional testing of a particular component that has proven to be prone to bugs in the recent past. Alternatively, it could decide to de-prioritize issues associated with software components that have not been used by customers (like a feature that exists in the software but is not currently enabled).

Summarizing, digitizing critical-to-quality processes open the door for a faster time to action on the customer experience. However, just like you can't build a house on quicksand, you must clean up existing processes before you are in a position to digitize. Like the digitization framework so clearly indicates, before you automate, you must streamline.

6.3.1.2 *Digitizing Customer Support*

Wouldn't it be great if the next time you go visit your doctor to check on a pain in your knee, he or she could quickly and unintrusively assess if you have other issues that need to be taken care of? The enabling capability would be a magical diagnostic machine that would scan your whole body and not only help you pinpoint your knee pain, but also identify what else might be wrong with you. Think of devices like the ones used by Dr. Crusher in the sick bay of the USS Enterprise in *Star Trek: The Next Generation*.

Unfortunately, back in today's customer support paradigm, companies tend to find out what is wrong with their customers from the customers themselves (i.e., customer calls). The focus is traditionally on training support engineers to ask the "right questions" of the customer during the call to enable the most expeditious diagnosis. Keeping the conversation focused on the issue at hand enables the engineer to tailor the line of questioning to a particular area and ultimately close the case quickly. The whole idea of getting into other potential issues with the customer is seen as counterproductive because it would only serve to divert attention from the current case and further delay its resolution.

Leading companies have begun to take advantage of digitization to start shifting the current paradigm. The new capabilities are seen as enabling the evolution of customer support into three specific strata:

1. *Better reactive support.* In reality, the path to predictive support could start with an ambitious support engineer taking advantage of additional configuration information already at his or her disposal as attachments to most customer cases. In this scenario, he or she would figure out that analyzing the data digitally would allow for faster troubleshooting. However, the support engineer would also quickly realize that such information could shed light on the health of the whole customer system. Suddenly, that broader scan would not only allow for faster troubleshooting of the original call, but also help identify what else might be lurking in the customer environment. That knowledge would not only help prevent future customer calls, but also—and more importantly—improve customer satisfaction.

    As a follow-up to the original concept, the technical support process could start by asking customers to upload certain information before they are connected to a live customer support person. By the time the support engineer joins the call, he or she would have an initial assessment of the customer situation based on the uploaded scan. This concept has already been widely adopted by credit card companies when you call customer support. Callers are asked to provide some identifying information (typically name and credit card number) through a robotic system; by the time agents come on the call live, they have the customers' profiles in front of them. Again, this capability allows a more accurate diagnostic and a faster time to resolution.

2. *Proactive support.* With the advent of telemetry, these leading organizations are looking to actively scan customer information. The goal is to detect potentially problematic situations and come up with customer-specific mitigation strategies. This capability allows a shift in the customer support paradigm from customer call–initiated to support engineer–initiated interactions. This would truly be proactive customer support.

3. *Predictive support.* Ultimately, we could envision a further evolution: a time when machine-learning algorithms are regularly performing health checks and when a vulnerability is detected, a mitigation action would be taken automatically. As the algorithms become more sophisticated, the system would be able to predict failures (even before they manifest themselves). This would usher in the arrival of the most advanced form of customer support: predictive support.

6.4 TELEMETRY DATA IN ACTION: CURRENT APPLICATIONS

In Chapter 3, we introduced the concept of adaptive customer experience. The idea is that access to real-time data and machine-learning algorithms would allow systems to interact with users and sense their experience and automatically adapt to improve it. While these concepts may seem dry and theoretical, we want to discuss four specific applications of telemetry-based technology.

These applications are available today and serve to illustrate the power of data telemetry to help improve the quality of our lives:

1. Fitness trackers

2. An artificial pancreas

3. Personal navigation systems

4. Magic bracelets

6.4.1 Fitness Trackers

Earlier in this text, we spoke about how one of the authors recently decided to start running to keep fit. After talking to some friends who are avid runners, he decided to buy a fitness-tracking device. At the very least, it helped him reinforce his commitment to running, even though he was not quite fully convinced. The device (see Figure 6.2) has the ability to track heart rate in real time, distance, path (using a global positioning system), cadence, elevation, etc.

At first, he would simply use the tracker to help understand his baseline through post-processing the data. How far did he run? How high did his heart rate go? What was the heart rate before he felt exhausted and had to stop? What is the recovery time? How steep was that climb? Answers to these questions helped him evaluate his performance and make structural adjustments (like tuning range, timing runs based on recovery time, figuring out how to best attack a climb, etc.). Also during this time, he discovered the capability to share runs with other running buddies. This helped create a support community that encouraged him when they saw he was trying to improve.

Then he started exploring semi-real-time capabilities like the ability to provide updates (through a paired smartphone and headphones) during the run. These updates include number of laps (or distance), average speed, and average heart rate. Using this information, he was able to apply corrections

Figure 6.2 Garmin 235 fitness tracker.

(slow down) if his heart rate was climbing too fast. This data really helped him get better "mileage" out of his current conditioning.

Finally, he discovered how to monitor the heart rate in real time by looking at the screen of the device and then applying fine corrections to his pace—at the moment—in order to maximize endurance. This in turn allowed him to build stamina and confidence so that, in the near future, he could run a marathon. In fact, he has successfully run a half marathon every month for the last three months!

This personal story is just one of many stories where users of this technology feel it has saved their lives. On September 22, 2015, ABC News reported the story of a 17-year-old boy whose fitness tracker saved his life.[5] This technology and its real-time telemetry data have definitely changed lives for the better worldwide.

6.4.2 An Artificial Pancreas

Similar wearable technology exists to help people diagnosed with Type 1 diabetes (also known as juvenile diabetes). This particular disease is triggered by the pancreas's inability to produce insulin, which in turn prevents glucose in the bloodstream from being consumed by the cells in the body. Consequently, even when a Type 1 diabetic eats, his or her body is unable to provide cells with the fuel necessary for normal function.

In order to manage this condition, Type 1 diabetics need to regularly inject insulin into their bodies to help process sugars in the bloodstream derived from food they have consumed (or will consume). Over the years, technology has been created to allow a small device called an "insulin pump" (see left side of Figure 6.3), which is attached to the body subcutaneously through a small plastic tube in order to deliver controlled amounts of insulin. The volume of insulin to be injected with every meal (called the "bolus") needs to be determined by the user through an offline analysis. This exercise estimates the required dosage of insulin based on the type of food and, more specifically, on the amount of carbohydrates the user has consumed (or will consume). Additionally, a separate "pinprick" blood test is required and a bolus is applied in order to establish the current baseline of blood glucose.

Later on, insulin pump technology was enhanced so that in addition to applying controlled amounts of insulin, insulin pumps can continuously track blood glucose through a second subcutaneous interface (see right side of

Figure 6.3   Original insulin pump and insulin pump with glucose monitoring.

Figure 6.3). This advancement eliminated the need for a separate pinprick blood test to establish the baseline, but carbohydrate estimation was still required.

Finally, a new technology called the "artificial pancreas" is in the process of being introduced in the U.S. market. It is called an artificial pancreas because it mimics the behavior of the pancreas as a regulator of glucose levels in the bloodstream. The artificial pancreas finally closes the loop for people with Type 1 diabetes by eliminating the need for an offline carbohydrate assessment. Instead, the artificial pancreas relies on real-time blood glucose measurements to determine the amount of insulin required. This technology greatly simplifies diabetes management and care for Type 1 diabetics and their loved ones and, at the same time, improves their life expectancy through better glucose control. This capability—powered by data telemetry—improves people's lives.

6.4.3 Personal Navigation Systems

Some of us are old enough to remember the days when long road trips always started by finding and studying a map. In fact, in preparation for the first road trip, one of the authors was encouraged by a friend to become a member of the American Automobile Association (AAA) and request a trip kit. Based on your destination, AAA would provide you a highlighted map that would trace your suggested route from your home to your destination and back. The map was a regular paper map (see Figure 6.4) with specific roads and highways highlighted. Sometimes it was a real challenge to read the fine print, and depending on your destination, you sometimes had to deal with dreaded "not on the map" situation.

The advent of electronic navigation systems for cars in the 1990s was a game changer. You simply entered your destination address and then, as if by magic, you were presented with turn-by-turn directions that could even be read aloud to you. No more paper maps! Even more impressive, the system estimated

Figure 6.4 AAA trip map.

the time to your destination based on average speeds and speed limits, so you could call Grandma and tell her the specific time you would be showing up for supper. Those of us using these systems at the time fondly recall the voice in the machine saying "recalculating" every time we made a wrong turn.

As smartphones became more and more popular in the 2000s, applications began to emerge that had the same functionality as the dedicated navigation systems. In fact, phones came with a built-in location capability that allowed them to trace a path to the destination starting from a non-postal address (i.e., the current location of the phone).

A further enhancement of the navigation applications was the introduction of real-time congestion monitoring. This capability allows users to avoid heavily congested portions of their route. The applications in real-time create alternative paths that are presented to the users for consideration if they are interested in rerouting. Systems also "remember" frequently used destinations and advises on estimated travel time as you leave your current location.

Today, personal navigation applications and associated information are pervasively used across the world. This data is not only used simply to trace paths to a destination, but to bring businesses and consumers together along the way. A perfect example of this is Uber, where customers use navigation data to identify potential rides. Once again, telemetry data has transformed people's lives and created a new market segment in the global economy.

6.4.4 Magic Bracelets

A few years ago, one of us was sitting in a large conference room with 300 or so colleagues participating in what is called an "offsite" meeting. Offsite meetings are a special type of meeting held by companies—typically off-premises, hence the name—to align everyone on a common strategy, look back on accomplishments, and look ahead at opportunities. It is customary to invite all members of the hosting organization to these events, and special guest speakers are brought in to share industry trends or innovations. Together, the authors have attended more than 200 of these events! However, this particular event is memorable because of the guest speaker. He was an executive from a theme park who came to present on customer experience trends. What he shared with the audience that day was fascinating!

The executive started his presentation by baselining how the company used to manage customer experience at its theme parks. The approach sounded very familiar because it involved a combination of both customer complaint analysis (here we go with our dependable customer calls) and customer survey analysis. He proceeded to describe all the metrics they have put in place over the years and how they govern those trends and use them to continuously improve customer experience. Then he talked about a pilot they were conducting based on a wearable capability he called the "MyMagic+" bracelet.[6]

What was this "MyMagic+" bracelet? As it turns out, this company had developed a wearable device (a bracelet) that could be handed out to guests as they entered the theme parks. This bracelet contained a unique radio-frequency

Figure 6.5 Disney's MyMagic+ bracelet.

identifier (RFID) associated with each particular guest, who could then use this device at specially configured scanning stations (see Figure 6.5) to check-in to rides, buy toys, pay for meals, and even open the door to his or her hotel room. As the guest scanned his or her bracelet at different places, each unique experience was tracked real time. This data allowed company engineers to build algorithms that would allow adapting the conditions to the guest's journey. For example, if, during a day, a person checked in to three rides and experienced more than a one-hour wait time on each, the company could create a fast lane for the person at his next ride. The point here is that the company was seeking to manage the guest's whole journey as opposed to point experiences.

The company later decided to operationalize this capability across all of its properties. We can only assume they were able to address concerns raised by personal privacy advocates. This constituency was worried about potential violations of personal privacy given the operator's ability to track people's movements across its facility. Regardless of the outcome of that debate, the use of wearable technology to trace people's journeys through the digital world is here to stay. Leading companies are learning how to capture this information and use it to create an adaptive customer experience.

6.5 TELEMETRY PROJECT CHECKLIST

If you are looking to implement and sustain a telemetry program in your organization, here are some items you need to consider. We will organize these into three categories:

1. Prepare

2. Create

3. Sustain

6.5.1 Prepare

Focus on understanding business value and establish a baseline of the current situation:

- Business
  - Have you identified the cross-functional stakeholders who would like to get involved in the telemetry journey?
  - Do you have a need to improve in certain areas based on feedback from your customers?
  - Do you have clarity on potential use cases and business value?
  - Do you understand which operational processes are involved?
  - Do you understand the level of digitization of existing processes?
  - Do you have the capability of implementing governance to oversee successful outcomes of the telemetry projects?

- Data
  - Can you describe the available data sets?
  - Do you understand the underlying characteristics of the data?
  - Do you understand the collection mechanism?
  - Do you have a data security and privacy policy?

- Infrastructure
  - Are you building your own or subscribing to data services?
  - If services, do you understand their security policies?
  - Do you have sufficient funding to build or buy?

- People
  - Do you have a chief digitization officer identified?
  - Do you have data scientists in the organization who can evaluate and assess the quality of the data?
  - Do you have resources to implement corrective actions based on data analyst recommendations?
  - Do you have change management experts to help drive adoption of insights?

6.5.2 Create

Focus on instantiating a new telemetry-based insights program in the organization:

- Business
  - Define a telemetry sponsor at a senior leadership level
  - Assign a telemetry project leader and begin working with stakeholders and creating use cases
  - If several functional teams are involved, identify the point of contact (POC) in each team with whom the leader can coordinate efforts to collect use cases from various POCs
  - Select IT resources to assist and partner with you
  - Prioritize use cases based on impact to business and ROI
  - Identify critical-to-quality processes and begin digitizing them

- Data
  - Identify who will receive the data and what will be done with the data
  - Define data architecture and schema by collaborating with IT
  - Create data policies
  - Create in-process metrics
  - Assign data stewards
  - Begin development of machine-learning algorithms

- Infrastructure
  - Consider technology options to realize your telemetry infrastructure
  - Build (or buy) a data lake
  - Initiate importing data

- People
  - Build a scrum team to begin working through use cases (user-story backlog)
  - Partner with the chief digitization officer on driving adoption and buy-in

If you have not started your telemetry journey, now is the time to begin. As demonstrated throughout this text, a telemetry-based infrastructure would help you understand:

- How customers are using your products

- Which features are used the most

- Which features are used the least

- Whether there is a failure or lingering issue that may negatively impact the customer before your customer calls

There has been a lot of technological progress in the field of telemetry and related tools. In this book, we discussed some of that progress. However, the technology is experiencing rapid change, and more efficient tools are constantly emerging in the marketplace. Our recommendation is that before you start implementing a change, conduct thorough research on the technology options available. Once informed, you need to determine the best solution to meet your needs and then confidently embark on your telemetry journey.

6.5.3 Sustain

Focus on ensuring that telemetry-based insights continue to be used in driving business outcomes and modified or deprecated if they are not. The data insights should be in the center of discussions for improving customer relations:

- Business
  - Create data governance framework
  - Integrate telemetry data insights into quarterly business reviews
  - Integrate telemetry data governance into the rhythm of the business

— Ensure a return on investment (ROI) analysis is conducted for all existing use cases
— Continue to identify additional use cases and maintain a prioritized list based on business impact/ROI

- Data
  — Implement data security protocols
  — Conduct regular data quality checks
  — Update/maintain master data management for telemetry
  — Define key practice indicators (KPIs) driven with telemetry data
  — Implement statistical process control for KPIs
  — Introduce machine-learning algorithms to accelerate time to action on insights
  — Develop training and tuning parameters for machine-learning algorithms

- People
  — Develop training programs around new telemetry insights, and ensure that new and existing personnel are continually trained on the value of telemetry for driving excellence in customer expectations and experience.
  — Implement a change management process and appropriate governance structure to obtain continual success
  — Ensure accountability is enforced for actions based on telemetry insights

The preceding checklists are provided as a sample to get you jump-started. You should customize the checklists based on your requirements and needs for the telemetry data. As you embark upon the journey, continue to refine the checklists to make them robust and current.

NOTES

1. John F. Kennedy, "Apollo expeditions to the Moon: Chapter 2," history.nasa.gov (1961), retrieved February 26, 2012.

2. Forrester Research Inc., "An executive primer to customer success management," April 2014.

3. Angel R. Martínez-Lorente, Frank Dewhurst, and Barrie G. Dale, "Total quality management: Origins and evolution of the term," *The TQM Magazine* 10, no. 5 (1998), pp. 378–386. doi:10.1108/09544789810231261.

4. "The Inventors of Six Sigma," archived from the original on November 6, 2005, retrieved January 29, 2006.

5. Emily Shapiro, "How an Apple Watch may have saved a teen's life," www.abcnews.com (2015), retrieved August 2, 2017.

6. Brooks Barnes, "At Disney Parks, a bracelet meant to build loyalty (and sales)," www.nytimes.com (2013), retrieved August 1, 2017.

Index

Note: Page numbers followed by *f* or *t* refer to figures or tables, respectively.

metrics for, 76–81, 89–90, 90*f*, 98–99, 156, 159–60
organizational visibility of, 105
productivity and growth of, 11–19, 11*f*, 71
products and services of. *See* products and services
research and development by, 6, 8
technology used by. *See* technology
telemetry used by. *See* telemetry; telemetry data; telemetry-enabled ecosystem; telemetry-enabled product development organizations
time to market, 5–6
websites of, 7

C

caching system, 123
calculators, 58
Callimachus, 58
Capability Maturity Model Integrated (CMMI), 84
Car2Go, 21
Cassandra, 62, 139
cause-and-effect identification, 26–27, 28*f*
Central Computer and Telecommunications Agency, 84
change management
   for anticipatory change, 28
   business practices impacted by, 134
   cultural change in, 133
   data protection and security obligations in, 134
   for directional change, 29
   forces against change, 31, 31*f*
   forces of change, 28*f*
   governing body responsibility for, 85
   implementation phases, 29–30
   for improvements, 27–31, 28*f*, 31*f*, 95. *See also* improvements
   for incremental change, 29
   for planned change, 29
   for proactive change, 85
   for reactive change, 85
   reasons for change, 28, 28*f*
   stages of change, 29–30
      management, 30
      preparation, 30
      sustaining, 30–31
   stakeholder buy-in to, 133–34
   storytelling or communication importance to, 95

for strategic change, 29
technology and system considerations for, 134
in telemetry-enabled ecosystem, 132–34
types of change, 28–29
checklists
   in root cause analysis, 26
   telemetry project, 168–71
chief data scientists, 73–74
chief digitization officers (CDOs), 157–59
classes of telemetry data, 59
classification of telemetry data, 68–70, 112, 116
closed loops
   cross-functional action teams in, 88
   customer experience improvements via, 81–96
   gap analysis for focus areas in, 89–90, 90*f*
   governing body in, 82–87
   key improvement area identification in, 87–88
   ongoing monitoring in, 96
   sustainability of improvements in, 90–96
cloud computing
   benefits of, 16
   considerations with, 16–17
   data structures/databases with, 61–62
   definition of, 16
   end device hosting via, 122
   ingestion points into, 123
   network virtualization and, 63
   private clouds in, 37
   productivity and growth via, 16–17
   public clouds in, 37
   storage via, 61–62, 63, 123, 124–25
combined product teams (CPTs), 88
communication
   improvement sustainability affected by, 95–96
   listening in, 89, 160–62
   storytelling as, 89, 95, 104, 108, 117, 119
companies. *See* businesses
conditional notifications, 124
confidential data, classification as, 69
configuration management, 85, 86
connectivity
   connected-product use cases, 44–45
   connectors creating, 125
   high costs of, 43–44
   telemetry creating connected customer experience, 41
consistency availability partition (CAP) theorem, 63, 63*f*

About the Authors

ALKA JARVIS

Alka Jarvis has 30 years of experience in software engineering, including 19 years spent in implementing quality management principles. Her background encompasses telemetry, cloud, IoT, customer experience, product and process quality, industry standards, corporate knowledge management, and training.

Cisco's first and only Distinguished Quality Engineer and a Fellow of American Society for Quality (ASQ), Alka has worked in a variety of capacities for Fortune 500 companies such as Apple, Bank of America, and AT&T, and she is a 22-year veteran of Cisco. A frequently invited speaker on quality assurance topics at international as well as domestic events, she has been an adjunct lecturer at Santa Clara University in computer engineering for the past 23 years. Her subject matter expertise is reflected in the eight books she has authored on the topics of customer experience and expectations, software engineering, quality management standards, and telemetry.

Alka is also an instructor for the software engineering courses at the University of California Santa Cruz and Berkeley extensions and won Silicon Valley's "Corporate Woman Advocate of the Year" award for her accomplishments in the software quality field. ASQ recognized Alka by publishing her achievements in their "Who Is Who in Quality" article.

In her role as the chair for nine years, representing the United States to the Technical Committee 176 for the International Organization for Standardization (ISO), she has been instrumental in the development of the 2000, 2004, 2008 versions of ISO 9001 and 9004 quality management standards. Alka was a member of the drafting committee and contributed in the writing of the latest ISO 9001:2015 version and is an ISO lead auditor, certified by Exemplar Global of United States for the past 23 years.

Named as an expert on Industry 4.0/Smart Manufacturing, she represented the American National Standards Institute (ANSI) and the United States in the strategic advisory group to the ISO's Technical Management Board at an international level.

Alka serves as the chair for the U.S. Standards Group Council; was a member of ASQ's Learning Institute Advisory Board; served as president of the Bay Area Quality Assurance Association (BAQAA); has been an Applied Total Quality Advisory Board member for University of California Berkeley Extension; an advisory board member to the Certificate Program in Continuous Improvement & Quality Management at the University of California Santa Cruz Extension; board member of the Quality Assurance Institute; an advisory member for ASQ's 2015 and 2016 International Conference on Quality Standards; and Vice President of Indian Business and Professional Women.

In her spare time, Alka enjoys mentoring and coaching students and young professionals to achieve their full potential in their aspirations. Having passion for food and fine wine, she spends endless hours on weekends discovering elegant restaurants in San Francisco and nearby Napa Valley with friends.

LUIS MORALES

Luis is an adjunct associate professor at Duke University's Pratt School of Engineering. He designed and teaches a software quality management class at Duke's Master of Engineering department. The class is designed to prepare students for a role in the software industry by providing techniques and experience in making the necessary tradeoffs to build software that meets customer expectations of quality. The class introduces students to five different business personas: customer, software engineer, software release/quality manager, customer support engineer, and general manager. The students can then appreciate the perspectives that each of these personas brings to its role and how that affects the "delivered" quality that customers actually experience.

Prior to teaching, Luis had a successful 28-year career as an engineering leader in the technology industry, including 13 years at Cisco and 15 years at AT&T. In his latest role at Cisco, Luis led a team responsible for quality insights. The team delivered quality insights as a service based on capabilities that included data and visualization, metrics and telemetry, descriptive and predictive analytics, and orchestration. The mission of the team was to create customer experience insights that compelled the business to act. The critical stakeholders included engineering, sales, and services leaders. He pioneered the adoption of a services-based architecture model for quality insights at Cisco.

In 2011, Luis and a few members of his team won Cisco's highest engineering innovation recognition, Cisco Pioneer Award, for work on the "Interactive Service Request Analyzer." This effort enabled the engineering organization to access service request data in order to drive continuous quality improvement for products.

Luis is coauthor of the book *Achieving Customer Experience Excellence through a Quality Management System*, published by ASQ Quality Press in 2016. He is an inventor with six U.S. patents in the areas of time and frequency, IP networking, and network security, and is a graduate of the University of California Berkeley in nuclear engineering.

When not teaching, Luis stays active learning or applying handyman skills, including landscaping, masonry, tiling, plumbing, electrical wiring, and welding.

He loves sailing at nearby lakes in his little Puffer sailboat. He enjoys cooking his specialty for friends and family, Paella Valenciana, based on a family recipe.

JOHNSON JOSE

Johnson Jose is a director at Cisco, accountable for engineering and supply chain business worldwide. He has over 17 years of extensive background in leading organizations, responsible for connecting Cisco's software pipeline all the way from customer requirement to end of life. In his current role, he manages Cisco's advanced analytics and data-driven predictive intelligence organization, which support R&D and supply chain quality orchestration.

He is specialized in software and supply chain digitization, with global footprint on key markets and geographies. He was responsible for several award-winning Cisco digital transformation projects with far reaching impact to Cisco's software vision. He is a well-known speaker in industry forums on the subject of software and supply chain digitization and method agnostic's development systems.

Johnson holds an engineering degree from University of Mangalore India, and an MBA in International Business from University of Wales UK. He is an alumina of HAAS School of Business, University of California Berkley. He is a certified executive coach with international coaching experience

Outside of work, Johnson enjoys travelling and is a keen observer of nature and human behavior. Being passionate about coaching, he sponsors and guides the young aspirants of Cisco's Early Career Network group.